SHOPPING FOR A BETTER COUNTRY

SHOPPING FOR A BETTER COUNTRY

Za Anku,
s najboljim željama!
Josip

Essays

JOSIP NOVAKOVICH

DZANC BOOKS

www.dzancbooks.org

These stories previously appeared in slightly different form and sometimes under different titles in the following publications: "Dead Fathers Society" in *World Literature Today*; "The Art of Coughing" in *Briar Cliff Review*; "Berlin Journal" in *Post Road*; "Blue Note" in *Opium*; "Five Easy Pieces in Moscow" in *St. Petersburg Review*; "Literary Tombs" in *Prairie Schooner*; "My Hungary" in *Nowhere Magazine*; "On Sleeping" in *Gihon Review*; "Ruth's Death" in *Boulevard*; "Shopping for a Better Country" in *Witness*; "Carthage, Algiers, and Fes" in *St. Petersburg Review*; "Sumka 43–A Captive Cello" in *Boulevard*; "Vukovar" in *Water-Stone Review*; and "Balkan Express" in *Boulevard*. The author is grateful to the journals' editors for publishing the essays and for granting reprint rights.

Book design by Steven Seighman

ISBN:978-1936873067

First edition: April 2012

Printed in the United States of America

10 9 8 7 6 5 4 3 2 1

For Eva, Jeanette, Joseph and other émigrés

CONTENTS

SHOPPING FOR A BETTER COUNTRY

SHOPPING FOR A BETTER COUNTRY

IN 1966, A MAN FROM MY HOMETOWN, whom I admired despite his certified insanity, managed to spend twelve hours abroad. He had cut the plywood above the toilet in the train from Zagreb to Vienna, and he crouched there for twenty-four hours. He had no sense of time, except that he knew it would have to take a long time to get abroad, to the free West. After twenty-four hours, he left his perch, expecting to be in Vienna, but he was where he started, in Zagreb. He had not seen Vienna, but the fact that he had been there made him exotic to me. This was his third attempt to escape Yugoslavia, for which he was rewarded by two years of treatment in the insane asylum. The official political reasoning was simple: if you wanted to leave a healthy society like socialist Yugoslavia to live in the decadent West, you were insane.

My older brother Vladimir, who later became a doctor, wanted to escape to Albania when he was twelve because he had heard that it was impossible to visit and leave Albania, so our father couldn't get to him there. Our father, a clog maker, exploited his older children for childhood labor, which was a normal thing in those days, but my older brother resented having to work four hours a day and not having any time for homework. Vlado hopped onto various trains, missing the direction entirely; he was returned by the police from the Austrian border after the entire family had begun to grieve for him, taking him for dead.

Later on, Vlado regretted that he hadn't emigrated right after his medical studies the way several of his friends did, becoming wealthy in Switzerland and the States. I had heard of men who were shot while trying to run across the border to Austria, but also of men who had managed to be smuggled out among potato sacks, and who later became prosperous Americans. The most famous émigré preceded our political system: Nikola Tesla. We had a saying: *Nikola Tesla sjeo na vesla, otiso u Ameriku i otkrio elektriku.* Nikola Tesla sat on a vessel, sailed to America, and discovered *elektrika*.

So it was my dream that when I grew up, I would emigrate, which seemed to be the ultimate achievement.

I wanted to be away from my country for many reasons. The popular quasi-folk music, with lots of wailing, tormented me. (This was long before Bregovic and Kusturica would make Yugoslav folk music fusion with gypsy and rock elements such a world-wide phenomenon.) I didn't like the communist propaganda (such as that we were unselfish people while the Westerners were warped by their greed), nor the constant ridicule of religion to which I was exposed as a Baptist. A history teacher once ordered me to stand up in front of the class and asked me, Are you selling opium? Don't you know it's illegal? What do you mean? I've never even seen the drug, I answered. You are selling religion to us; don't you know that Marx said, Religion is the opiate of the masses? Religion is for cowards.

There were only three thousand Baptists in the entire country, and we were regarded as sectarian zealots; the law prohibited proselytizing in public places, yet what is a Baptist without proselytizing? Now I resented the church as well for pushing me into compromising situations (such as the public conflict with the teacher) and for trying to excommunicate me when my friends and I formed a rock band. I wanted to be away from my home church just as much as I wanted to be away from our socialist state, which boasted of "the dictatorship of the proletariat."

However, going abroad proved to be easier than I had imagined. To resolve unemployment problems and to attract hard currencies, Tito opened up our borders and allowed Yugoslavs to go abroad as guest workers in Germany and France. In 1976, I went to Vassar College as a transfer student, and remained in the States to study religion and philosophy at Yale. In the college dining halls, whenever my fellow students learned I was from Yugoslavia, they almost invariably asked me how I managed to escape. They expected me to be an exile, and my tale of easy and legal departure in the role of a student seemed to be a letdown. Moreover, repeating the same answer bored me—I believed conversation should above all be entertaining—so I came up with stories of swimming across the Drava River under gunfire. The second question, which usually followed, was: Is your family still in Yugoslavia? What do you mean by still, I'd snap back. Not everybody plans to come to America.

I felt offended that my country was put down like that, and wanted to offend my fellow conversationalists' assumptions of political and cultural superiority vis-à-vis the East.

Away from Yugoslavia, suddenly I found it in many ways more appealing than before. I had hoped to encounter a lot of rock and jazz in the States, and instead heard disco everywhere. Instead of communes and conversations about free love and peak experiences, I often entered predictable conversations about communism vs. capitalism. The sheer unquestioning simplicity of the widespread American patriotic narcissism put me on guard. Whenever I walked off campus, I saw many American flags, more flags per square mile than anywhere else.

What my fellow students found incredible, however, was my new plan to go back to Yugoslavia after spending a few years in the States. They stared at me as though I was crazy, and a friend of mine, a pre-med student and son of an orthopedic surgeon, well supplied with all sorts of pain killers and other drugs, concluded that since I was so insane I wanted to go back to communism, I needed treatment: first talk therapy, and then drug therapy, morphine, pot, speed, and if all else failed, acid.

That Americans on the average seemed to be patriotic put me off. At school and at home in Yugoslavia, I was taught not to distinguish between patriotism and nationalism; the word patriotism was an attempt to present the same ugly nationalist phenomenon of favoring your country over others; patriotism was a patriarchal swindle that made it easy to recruit soldiers to shed the blood of other peoples. In our socialist education, nationalism was equated not only with the bourgeoisie but also with Nazism, and Croatian nationalists, invariably, with Ustashas, the Croatian fascists who committed many atrocities in the Second World War. Yugoslavia was constantly on guard against Croatian and Serbian nationalists. who could blow up theaters and commit other acts of terrorism, as they occasionally did.

In elections in America, everybody had to prove their patriotism above all, which seemed strange to me. I was raised with the slogan, Workers of the World Unite, and the idea that it was progressive to be international. Here one had to be reactionary, regressive, to pass muster as a politician. The requisite and unquestioning love of the Constitution, the Bill of Rights, and the flag struck me as very similar to the Christian fundamentalist love of the Bible and the Cross, but even more dogmatic.

I had no serious reason to fear going back to Yugoslavia at that time, and I was tempted to go back. Yugoslavia was a prosperous country—with the highest standard of living in the Communist Bloc—like America would be at the beginning of the third millennium in the West. Yugoslavia had borrowed a lot of money from the International Monetary Fund and wasn't returning it yet, nor intending to return it. (Does America really intend to return fourteen trillion dollars, our national debt, owed mostly to foreign banks?)

However, Yugoslav prosperity seemed to be temporary. Tito was ill, and there were speculations that the country would fall apart violently as soon as he died. The slogan there was, After Tito, Tito. We were raised on many slogans, such as Brotherhood and Unity, and after being brainwashed for twenty years, I actually believed that Yugoslavia was a solid country even for a few year's after Tito's death, until ethnic bickering intensified in the late 80's.

Since I could return to Yugoslavia but remained in the States, I was actually in voluntary exile, which had some psychological similarities to a real, involuntary one. It wasn't exactly a luxury exile because I never had much money, and prior to getting a green card I had no right to work. Since I was lazy, it was actually a good excuse not to take up any jobs but to scheme how to remain a student. When I visited rich acquaintances of mine in Seattle and we rode in a jeep into the mountains, everybody contributed for gas and food but I didn't. Later, three people complained to one of them, who was closest to me, that they had grown to hate me because I never paid for anything; I was an exploiter. Now I can see their perspective. At that time I was filled with financial self-pity. I envied them that they could afford to go to one of the last Led Zeppelin concerts, and I couldn't afford a ticket. I envied that they could go to a restaurant—I could eat only bread with milk from the stores. I was skilled in not spending money. I had hitchhiked to Seattle, and would hitchhike back to New Haven.

I couldn't afford hotels, so I slept in bushes near churches in my travels, and in Boise I was so tired that I slept in the middle of the street like an alcoholic (though I couldn't afford a drop, and at the time had no interest in drinking). In front of a bank, in the center of town, I sprawled on the warm summer asphalt and slept for five hours, and nobody bothered me.

I probably could have gotten odd jobs, but I was scared that the INS would find me out and I would be thrown out of the country. No identity information was computerized yet, and the system was loose—there were many illegal immigrants, seven million, according to the *New York Times* estimates. This was before the amnesty program to offer permanent residency to many illegal aliens.

I finished my studies at Yale Divinity School and continued my education as a graduate student in philosophy, in the Ph.D. program, because I didn't know how to get a job or even how to work. Having been raised in the worker's state, I was a shirker rather than a worker until I dropped out of school and got a green card.

My saga of being an immigrant is neither a touching one nor a difficult one. I enjoyed hanging out in this country. I never considered myself to be an exile. My fellow students, professors, coffee-shop acquaintances in New York—nearly all of them asked me how it was to be an exile from the Communist Bloc, and I usually answered that I was not an exile, that I would return to Yugoslavia to become a psychiatrist—that I was sufficiently screwed up to become a psychiatrist.

Later, when I began to publish books with Graywolf, I didn't talk with my publicist about the details of my biography, and she put on the cover, "Croatian-born writer-in-exile." I guess that sounded good to her, and it was too late for me to complain and make her job miserable, so I let it pass. The word exile was supposed to be magnetic, to validate what I was saying, to lend the heft of suffering to my otherwise frequently satirical and silly writing. Yet I hated to see the word applied to me. I knew I had not earned it. At the same time, suddenly there were many exiles from Yugoslavia as the country was falling apart and going to hell.

I didn't know that even my mother would be an exile. She took a night train to Switzerland where my brother Ivo lived and studied theology at a Baptist seminary—she wasn't in a camp but still she couldn't go back to our hometown as long as it was under Serbian siege. My sister-in-law's mother was there as well; she felt threatened as a Serb in my hometown. My mother felt threatened as a Croat. And the two poor women were so much under the sway of these perceived and misperceived threats that they had many political arguments and had to be separated, placed in different rooms, to guarantee peace.

I returned to Croatia to see what was happening there. I had to go through UN checkpoints; the bus I rode in sported several bullet holes. I saw houses set on fire and visited relatives with howitzer holes in the walls of their homes. They refused to become exiles. The experience of smoke, fire, tanks, checkpoints, felt exilic enough, however. By not going anywhere, they were more displaced than they would have been by shifting into the comfort zone of a prosperous country. An old man near my hometown claimed that he had no need to travel. He had lived in eight countries and in one house. He remained faithful to the previous regimes, and thus felt like an exile most of his life, without going to the train station. He still loved the Hapsburg Emperor Franz-Josef.

It is quite likely that I have gone through fewer real changes than that old man in my hometown. I could live in several countries yet remain in essentially the same mental landscape. Maybe I have not become an American. Incidentally, I just gave a talk in Moscow, an event sponsored by the Croatian Embassy and American Cultural Center, and a man in the audience asked me whether I could feel like simply an American and be aloof from the Balkans while the war was taking place. I answered, On the contrary. The war affirmed that I could never be simply an American, that I would always also be Croatian and even Yugoslav, and that I was far from aloof, but had obsessively suffered the news from the war on the short wave radio, newspapers, internet, phone, and in person, traveling there as much as possible.

The United States used to be the perfect country for exiles, second best after France. In France, you could be an exile with style, and fit perfectly in the café culture; if you came from Eastern Europe, you wouldn't be considered a social inferior but Bohemian, an ally against the Germans, and so on. In Germany and Austria, my impression was that you couldn't feel comfortable as an exile because of chauvinism, particularly North vs. South. I could speak German fluently, and during my month-long visit to Vienna, a man in a tavern commented, So, you are a Yugoslav but intelligent. It was both a compliment and an insult—a compliment to me and an insult to my original country. I never felt that kind of chauvinism in the States—people didn't expect me to be stupid simply on account of coming from Eastern Europe. Here, it was still Europe, not the second-hand Europe, Slave Europe, even if it was Slav. For Germans, Croats and Serbs were mostly cheap labor, despicable lower-class trash.

In most of Western Europe, I couldn't be a European. In Germany and Austria, people laughed on several occasions when they learned I was from Yugoslavia. Dutch people on a train laughed about Yugoslavia, and had some filthy anecdotes about bathrooms to retell. My sister lived in Germany for thirty years, working as a cardiac clinic nurse, and she speaks better German than Croatian, but she never feels at home there. She is still a *Gastarbeiter,* guest worker, no matter what.

———

Maybe, like that old man near my hometown who had lived through eight different regimes, I could remain in one place and see how it changes. The States are changing. Strangely enough, I am beginning to feel like an exile when I go to a polling station in PA and people hold placards approving attacking Middle Eastern countries, supporting the troops. Imagine if in Nazi Germany people said, Look, we know the war is wrong, but we love our boys and we support them. It's the wrong time to withhold our support now that they are struggling for German ideals, defending Auschwitz. The comparison is extreme, but why support the troops in an unsupportable war?

I feel like an exile when I think of going to the hospital and see what the bills would be. Recently, I took an AIDS test at State College in Pennsylvania because that was a requirement to go to Russia for half a year as a Fulbright fellow. The secretary was alarmed that I wanted to take the test, and she even declined to test my wife unless she first went through psychological counseling. Jeanette said, Wait a minute, this is simply for a visa requirement. The check-in person and the nurse didn't believe her. The level of suspicion is high now in the States. When I talk on the phone with my brother Ivo, who is a theology instructor at Baylor, he invariably wants to talk politics, and I hear clicking in the background, and I say, Why talk politics, just remember where we are!

I used to have that experience with my older brother Vlado in Yugoslavia: I would want to expound my political views, but he would point to the phone, and say, Why talk politics, remember where we are. This is not America. How things have changed! Now I tell my brother Ivo, Remember where we are. This is not Croatia!

Now I am tempted to say, Remember where we are. This is not America. We as Americans are being exiled from our country of liberty through the general paranoia being injected into our asses. The total spying which we suspected in Yugoslavia, Hungary, and East Germany, is only now possible, in the States, through credit cards, computers, EZ passes, surveillance cameras, and well-meaning neighbors. We can be observed. But as a friend of mine points out, So what? What has happened to you? Who can review and read all that data?

Nothing has happened to me, I say, except that I feel self-conscious now. I am not doing anything bad, but I feel self-conscious, the way I did as an adolescent, when I danced relatively spontaneously but then saw myself in the mirror, and my dancing looked awful and I no longer wanted to do it. Maybe my conversation and my emails sound awful, and I should like to quit communicating. But I refuse to feel self-conscious. I will write the way I please, I will talk the way I please—or at least I hope so.

Countries change, of course, and it is still the same country, in a way, resembling a McCarthy America, except that McCarthy's America was not in debt. This is a bankrupt America, bankrupted partly by its suspicions and overspending on the military and over-reliance on consumerism.

So how much do I belong to America? This is my chosen country. Was, anyway. Croatia is my rejected country, was anyway. And now? How do I define my nationality? Do I need to? I often refuse to, but then I am introduced as a Croatian writer, or American, or Croatian-American. I don't lose sleep over the definition, but nevertheless, the problem is there. (And to further complicate it, I am emigrating to Canada!)

The question of nationality remains a question no matter how I answer it. If a nation rejects you and you reject it, it still is not a permanent and absolute severance of ties. It's like disowning parents when you are fifteen and then weeping at their funeral when you are fifty. That is what a friend of mine, a Serbian exile from my hometown in Croatia, has done. Miodrag disowned his father, but he found his father's death very painful and fears that he might be like his father and commit suicide one day. He also disowned Croatia, but now he plans to retire there. Of course, after Yugoslavia fell apart, Miodrag has two or three homelands, one where he immigrated, Great Britain, one where he grew up, Croatia, and the other, Serbia, where he studied and got married for the first time (he's been married three times, I believe), and although he doesn't visit Serbia, he might still reclaim that homeland as well. Now in his successive polygamy with women and with nations there's a striking parallel. You can divorce, but if you have children with someone, you never fully do. You can leave the country of your birth, but you never fully do.

Anyhow, for a while I wanted to be fully American, and believed that America was a cosmopolitan, multinational and transnational country, and I believed in the Marxist notion that nationality is a purely bourgeoisie phenomenon which willdisappear with the disappearance of the classes. But the classes are not disappearing, and these days, there are sharper divides between the rich and the poor all over the world. While the rich may feel global enough and have enough of a global reach through travel and finance, the poor and even the middle class seem to be stuck where they are, and their identity depends on where they are. If they are in America and have been there most of their lives, they are American; if they are in Russia, they are Russian, etc. No matter what, even if nations suddenly disappear, they would still exist for me since I grew up with them; they would remain a significant part of my psychology as so much of my thinking and remembering and activity has had to do with leaving one country for another, and with choosing to become an American citizen, and choosing to write in English rather than in Croatian.

Who are you? people asked me in Russia, at the Murmansk Writers' Club. You've been introduced to us as an American writer but we see you are Croatian.

I am both.

When you left, did you feel that you betrayed your country? a writer at the round table asked me.

No, I felt that my country betrayed me since I couldn't fit in as a Protestant.

Ah, so, said the writer, now I understand. That's how you can live in America. I am sure I couldn't.

But nation is not the same thing as religion, is it? I asked. You can be a Catholic and still be a Russian, you can be Jewish, Muslim. . . and still be Russian.

Then you have two identities, and you betray one.

I have two identities, and having them makes me more American than not having them would make me. And perhaps America is unique that way, that dual identities are part of most people's heritage.

A woman stood up and said, I have visited Croatia, and it is the most beautiful country in the world. How dare you leave it! You should be ashamed of yourself. And isn't it true that most Americans are fat and stupid?

(Wow, I thought, how things have changed. Where is the American prestige? And why indeed did I leave Croatia?)

Listen, I answered her. America used to be a great country. It has declined, I admit. I couldn't predict that.

Now, if I decided suddenly to forget about the rest of the world and become a Russian, could I be a Russian at the age of fifty? I don't think so. They might accept me as a Slav, via the nebulous Slavic soul, but for me, despite long immersion in Russian literature and culture, it still wouldn't work. If I were younger, sure. I could be an expat in Russia, but an expat has a patria. It's not the ex but the patria that defines you. The question is which patria is stronger, the new or the ex—or is it all about having an ex, and the exing? The act of leaving gives us expats the real sense of identity and home—of nomad home.

Now, after living in the States for thirty years and having American kids, I have sort of earned the identity, but America, now in a state of disarray, with its huge suburbia, huge cars, and ugly, unwalkable downtowns, has suddenly alienated me. I feel more at home in Russia, where I can walk into chaotic streets, where many people walk. But feeling at home and being part of a place is not the same thing.

I perhaps thrive in this national confusion. The tongue has much to do with it. I have chosen English and lived in it so long that it has become my home. No matter where I go, I have this English. Of course, I have Croatian as well, but I don't write in it, I read in it very little, and I talk in it rarely.

The question of exile and national identity can't cease for me. Some people know where they belong. My mother, although born in Cleveland (where she lived until she was three years old), knows she belongs in Daruvar, Croatia, where she spent most of her life. Despite possible hesitations in identity, she had—thirty-five years ago, to my horror—her name cut into the gravestone next to my father's, after my father's death. She did not remarry, and now she seems to be dying. For a while she had a strong pull toward America, and one year she wanted to fly there to see the country, but I was too broke to buy her a ticket, and just a few years later, when I could finally afford to buy one, she did not want to go. She did not feel up to it, and her desire subsided. Still, to my mind she could belong in Cleveland Calvary Cemetery, Lot 111, where her Slovenian immigrant grandmother is buried. But she does belong more to Daruvar, where actually, as I rewrite this essay, she is already buried, in the soil where I was born, only two kilometers away, and where most naturally I will be buried when it comes to that, as that indeed is my native soil. Actually, I have no idea where I will be buried.

Chopin, famously, as an exile from Poland, kept a bit of Polish soil, *rodna gruda,* native soil, in a jar and wept over it. Was he ever French? His name is pronounced the French way: Shop-Un, not Hop-In (as it is in Polish). He became

French and remained Polish—although his remains are at Père Lachaise buried under French soil and an incessant supply of flowers from Polish visitors.

Some people are practically unexileable. For example, Solzhenitsyn, while in Vermont, was in Vermont only physically. He recoiled from anything American—the disco music particularly horrified him—and continued to write about Russia, and as soon as he could, he returned to Russia. Well, he is now buried there, in Rodina.

Nabokov, on the other hand, loved being an American, and waved his American passport proudly when he traveled in Europe. Yet, rather than weep for the native soil, he tended to weep for the native language, writing pages and pages of the untranslatable nuances of his favorite Russian words.

While I used to be proud to show my American passport, now I am a bit more hesitant, and I might be shopping for a better country. I enjoyed immigration to the States, writing in English, and if I were younger, I would perhaps look for a third language to write in, exile myself spiritually. Now, in 2011, I am thinking of moving to Montreal, living at least with the presence of another language in my ears. Maybe it's a waste of energy to worry about it all, and maybe it's simply a longing for a change of political and cultural scenery that drives me to seek yet another shift in my nationality.

I think for me the essence of emigration, of being an émigré, is that I have not resolved the issue of national identity and that I never could. My coming to America took place too long ago; it has lost its freshness. I am tempted by the possibility or impossibility of another shift in identity. That shifting may be more important than the concrete choice of where to move and what national belonging to strive for.

For me the issue of being an émigré, or exile, or *Gastarbeiter*, boils down to border crossings physically and mentally; being an émigré depends on breaking down the borders and definitions of national identities. I am exiled from easy definitions, from clear identity. Exiled from exile, but not from migration, emigration and immigration. Who am I? It would be best if I could answer, *Mensch*, citizen of the world. Or maybe a Canadian in the making? Could I begin to think of myself as Canadian? How long would it take? Or if I moved to Canada, would I suddenly be reminded of just how American I was? (Actually, since writing this I have moved to Canada and I am working on my Canadian immigrant papers, and I suddenly feel more American than ever. . . after all, I was naturalized in the States, sorry to say. Canada has been voted the country with the best reputation in the world by the Reputation Institute— that institute actually sounds pretty disreputable to me—and maybe in many ways it is, but I don't have that impression yet as I have to file incessant paperwork, worse than I remember in Yugoslavia and perhaps even Russia.)

Moving away from Croatia made it easier for me to write about Croatia. I have written more about Croatia than about any other place, and in a way, my being in America has strengthened my being Croatian. I have difficulties writing about the States—not that it is a boring country, but perhaps I need the distance, and there's a lot to say. Now, in Canada, maybe I will discover that I have more to say about America and more to remember and imagine than I suspect? I do suspect! As a good American, I suspect. In God we trust, and suspect everybody else.

DEAD FATHERS SOCIETY

THE MATH IS SIMPLE: men marry older and die younger than women. That means that many children born to older parents grow up with a dead father lurking in the background. My father died when I was eleven. One of the first things I want to find out when I meet people is whether they lost their fathers. I think there is camaraderie among the people who lose their fathers early. I experienced that as soon as my father died; I made friends with a boy who seemed to hate me before.

The day after my father died Mladen and I stood kicking stones in my backyard, and he said, Now we are the same.

What do you mean?

My father died when I was three. You will see what it's like not to have a father.

He seemed gleeful to have a friend in the same predicament, and while I can't say I rejoice to find out someone had lost his father early on, I do feel immediate camaraderie on that account.

I take this camaraderie into the writing world, where I notice which writers lost their fathers in their youth. My friend, Bill Cobb, lost his at the age of four. The first novel Bill wrote opens with an image of a father's ear pickled in a jar, for remembrance—a beautiful and macabre image. I think that describes the sensibility of many of us, male or female, in this non-exclusive club, the dead fathers club. Another friend of mine, Madelon Sprengnether, describes in her book, *Crying at the Movies*, the moment that sent her adrift into her youth and adulthood: she saw her father drown in the Mississippi. He slipped off a sandy islet while saving his son, and an undertow pulled him in, and to Madelon's horror, he didn't resurface. When I visited her she was listening to Mahler, some of the most tragic-sounding passages. You sure know how to spread cheer, don't you, I asked her. She laughed. I like grief, I find it beautiful. OK, that is slightly twisted, but then, I agreed with her. Those jolts in minor keys, they do something electrifying for my brain, too. Of course, it would be too much to claim that the others who haven't lost their fathers early don't know such pleasures of grief.

At a certain level, when I get together with friends who have lost their fathers, I have the sensation of being in a group of kids who are playing without supervision. The supervisor, the builder of the super-ego, has vanished. Sure, he lingers on in a ghostly and sometimes intimidating way.

It's possible that in moments of fear, I clung to the super-ego, as though it could give me the security of being with a father the protector. To this my faith in God was easily grafted, and sure, in moments of danger, I prayed to God, but in moments of pleasure I shunned God. My father died in such a way that he only strengthened my fear and my faith. The fear of God is the beginning of wisdom, the Biblical saying goes, and seeing my father die filled me with dread and with a desire to transcend it.

In 1968, February 6, midnight, both my brother and I finished our shrieks of horror upon seeing blood coming out of Father's nose after his heart attack, and upon feeling no pulse in his hand and neck, yes, after our frantic prayer to God to save him, we paused, almost surprised that we were alive ourselves. And what now? I asked. My brother Ivo stared at me with incomprehension—that life would go on. For a few seconds we were both calm, strangely relieved. A horror could happen, and you could go on. Soon we relapsed into wailing and prayers, and when I tried to go to bed, I shivered. (Well, it was a winter night, and I am not sure we remembered the heat.)

My relatives and family friends who came to pay homage to my father's corpse, which was laid out on a table in the living room, looked at me with sympathy, petted me on the head. I hadn't felt loved that much before. I slipped away from the party into the yard, and there, the thought that I was free startled me. Who could catch me now? I could run away, I could do something bad, and there would be no father to flog me (he believed in the biblical don't spare the rod). There would be no father to judge me. Nobody else's judgment had mattered that much. Who should judge me now? My mother? Sure, but she was milder, and she was consistently cynical, so that if she said something negative, it didn't matter—I was used to it. She would whip me with her words, not with a rod, and words would leave no wounds but self-doubt.

I came back into the house to mourn, but I had this dirty secret, that at some level beyond and beneath all the horrors, I was pleased. But that didn't last. The fear—How will we live now? Will we be poor? Will we have enough to eat?—came to the fore. Who will run our father's clog-making workshop? Even before then, we could afford to eat meat only once a week; the rest of the week we ate vegetable stews, dark wheat bread, and eggs.

My brother and I were known to be good fighters among the kids in town. Almost every day we were involved in fistfights, wrestling matches, and so on, many for sport, as a test of strength and skill, and many out of conflicts of pride, or a sense of justice (if I saw a boy torturing a cat, I would attack him). Soon after the death of my father, I had a fight which I thought I should win, but suddenly I got scared that I would lose, and I was too slow, so I found myself under the boy, who was hitting my head against the cement of the handball stadium. I lost another fight soon afterward. This loss of self-confidence may not be universal with the loss of a father, but it does seem to be fairly common. My brother went through the same crisis. He quit fighting and began to play the guitar. He hid himself in the attic and played for hours; he wanted to become a classical guitarist but there was not enough support for that. He became excellent nevertheless, and was invited to play with one of the best rock groups in Yugoslavia, but he admitted that he didn't show up for the first concert because of stage fright. Maybe he could have become a rock star, but his doubts drove him back to the attic. He dropped out of the fancy grammar school where he was enrolled and became a factory worker, and later, he became philosophical, and pursued his introverted activities to such an extent that he just got a Ph.D. in Theology from the Princeton Theological Seminary. He is almost certain that his life path would have been different if our father had lived past our adolescence. Well, our older brother, who was twenty-seven at the time of our father's death, had become a doctor, a far more practical man than the two remaining brothers.

Of course, my theory is subjective, and I wouldn't be surprised if a sociological study proved my common sense wrong. Before my father's death, I didn't have a practical bent anyway. I wasn't one of those guys who at the age of seven knows exactly what he wants to do with his life and proceeds to do it, like Tesla, who had a clear image of putting a turbine generator into Niagara Falls, and did just that thirty years later.

When I visit friends who have fathers, I'm usually surprised. Sometimes I wonder why one would want to hang out with an old guy. Hardly any of my friends' fathers have struck me as anchors of stability and wisdom. Maybe I don't make friends with people who have strong fathers, but more likely there are very few strong fathers. It's hard to be a good father. I know it, because I'm a father. Actually, now my son is as old as I was when my father died. Sometimes, jokingly, I tell him to be nice to me because you never know—fathers just don't last.

His name is basically the same as mine, except that mine is Josip, the Croatian version of Joseph, and his is the English. My father's name was Josip as well. I know in many traditions it's considered bad luck to name your son the same name as yours, but I don't think I had much choice; there are so few traditions in my family, it's easier to break one than to create one or keep one. My father's father was Josip, and his father was Josip; that one was killed by a tree when my grandfather was only three years old.

My father apparently didn't feel like continuing the tradition to name the eldest son Josip, so he named my brother Vladimir. Another, he named Ivan, and then when I was born, my father pondered what the hell to name me. My mother wasn't interested in naming me since I had given her too much pain in childbirth; she nearly died. That was before C-sections. So Vladimir told my father, You forgot something.

And then he remembered. Oh, of course.

And so, thanks to that crazy tradition, to see what my tombstone will look like I go to the cemetery and see my father's, with Josip Novakovic clearly inscribed in silver letters.

When you have a father, you learn how to become a father. At first, I was excellent friends with my son, but lately we have our problems. He can't stand it if I win at ping-pong or chess. I tell him, what would you like me to be, a loser? I played this game for thirty years and you for thirty days and you already want to beat me? When he was six I taught him how to play soccer, and if I scored more than he did, he cried, so I had to pretend that I was trying but would have to let him win if I wanted him to continue. Then we went to a soccer practice at his grade school. I did the same thing with the boys in school, when I was a goalie for a joke. I let a ball pass by me into the net. My son cried. I said, what's wrong? It turned out he believed that I was the best soccer player in the world, invincible, and that a kid could score on me seemed to him insufferable. He had just lost the image of an invincible father, and that shook him up. Of course, that he could score against me would make him the best player, and my letting others score not only devaluated my image but also his.

How necessary are fathers? Most mammalian families don't include fathers. At the essential biological level, father is not a necessity, mother is. Maybe it's a matter of evolution that gives humans an edge to have a father assist with feeding and protection, but even so, in the early stages of civilization, fathers usually didn't hang around that much. They were out hunting, waging wars, engaging in risky activities that frequently resulted in their early deaths. And when they died, other men could take over the protective functions for the tribe, of hunting and waging wars. In old Hebrew marriage laws, if a man died, his brother was to take over the role of husband to the widow. So, a specific father is dispensable. A father who always stayed at home was perhaps a blocker of development for kids; with his presence, perhaps the male children aren't propelled into work and independence quite so quickly as without him.

Despite the sense of uncertainty that losing my father gave me, I found out that I was more independent now, freer. I could use my father's absence to my advantage. When I was 12, I was about to be excommunicated from the Baptist church because of several incidents—growing long hair, smoking cigarettes, and stealing empty wallets at the town fair. I missed many meetings, and during prayer meetings I refused to pray. The tyrannical minister came to me and said that because I didn't have a father, the church elders had decided to give me another chance. If I needed a father, he'd act as one. I thanked him for the offer. In retrospect, that sounds like Bush's offer to Putin to bring democracy to Russia.

At school, I skipped many classes. For a while, I'd walk toward the school, circle around it in the park, and walk on into the forest, and spend the whole day climbing trees and reading. My poor attendance was excused since I didn't have a father. The house was quieter now. I could afford to be lazy. I didn't have to play musical instruments. But my brother, who refused to play while the father was alive, now played like crazy. . . as though to invoke father back.

I remember many comforts of having a father. He used to sing occasionally, in the evening, accompanying himself on a guitar. He played the violin, tambourine, double bass, and several other instruments. He told us stories—maybe not many times, maybe only half a dozen times, but that left a great impression on me—about Dugonja, Vidonja, i Trbonja (the tall one, the seeing one, and the fat one). He improvised quite a bit. Each of his trips turned into a tea time, and while the rest of us chewed bread with honey and butter, he told us how he, with the help of his heavenly father, got out of many dangers. Maybe my writing has something to do with both his absence and the lingering sound of his stories, the most impressive of which was the trip to the other world, when his heavenly father did not intercede to get him out of the dangers of his heart.

I grew interested in storytelling perhaps because Father was a fantastic storyteller. He knew long segments of the Bible by heart, and now I kept reading the Bible, as well as Alexander Dumas, Karl May, and the *Iliad* and the *Odyssey*. Maybe the world of imagination and myth brought me close to the absent father.

My father's death gave me an impetus to write. Upon reading *The Death of Ivan Illych*, I thought I could describe my father's death, and I wrote two hundred pages of sketches involving our backyard and streets of my hometown, yet I couldn't write about his death, and instead began to write a satirical story about dying, a comedy of sorts. Later I wrote a few poems about him and his dying and my dreams of him as still alive and dying for the second and the third time. I wrote a couple of essays about his death, and an autobiographical story, which got me my first serious publication, in the Discovery issue of *Ploughshares*. And my novel, *April Fool's Day*, has a long segment, a description of a strange death, which, I am sure, came out of my father's death.

So writing is my patrimony. Even this essay is. Or at least I imagine so, perhaps wishing to give my father a role in my life, so that even his absence is a form of ghostly presence.

TERRIBLE TWOS TRAVEL

To TAKE OUR SON JOSEPH out in public meant stress, for the parents and for the public. We could not in good conscience take the little savage to Burger King, let alone to a good restaurant, because he'd scream, toss fries and juice on the floor, and, once he had the attention of the chewing audience, grab his mother's bra and pull it, exposing her breast, with the war cry *Milka!* So when my wife, Jeanette, suggested that we take a trip to Europe, and take Joey along to Zurich, Paris, and Venice, I wanted to say no, but didn't. I became the yes-man, and Joey, of course, was the no-man (*outis*), and I'm sure that if he'd had a say in the matter, he would have said no. Since he was a month short of two, his airfare would be only ten percent of the regular fare. This was our last chance to go to Europe as a family and not go bankrupt.

Soon after our decision, Jeanette and I, Joey, and two French friends of ours sat in a corner table near the entrance on the second floor of a restaurant near the Bastille in Paris. Although it was warm, Joey insisted on wearing his woolen ski cap and his blue mittens. He played with a bulldozer and a dump truck, little orange metal toys. He giggled, hugged a bottle of wine, lifted it and panted, as though he were weight-lifting, and said, "Wine, Mama, that's wine!" He was proud that he could identify and name things.

The dinner conversation about world politics did not go smoothly because Joey often interrupted, calling for milk and for trucks. To keep him quiet, we called a *garçon*, and asked for chocolate. "We have only black chocolate for cooking," he said. He brought a little plateful of chocolate shavings. Joey tasted a little, spat it out. We wiped the spot he hit on the white tablecloth. "Dirt," Joey said. But he did not mean anything bad by that. Dirt was the most precious material to him. With his bulldozer he pushed chocolate shavings from the plate onto the tablecloth and across it. Once he had a streak of chocolate on the table in front of him he stood in his chair, grabbed the steamroller and rolled over the chocolate, grinding it into the tablecloth. He was paving the road.

"Don't do that!" I said.

"What's the alternative?" Jeanette said. "At least he's quiet and happy. Better than if he screamed."

We looked anxiously around, to see how the waiters would take this. A waiter walked away briskly. Trouble. He came back with another plateful of chocolate shavings because Joey was running out. Soon Joey was building a cross-highway, his ski cap on, his tongue licking a corner of his mouth, his mittens on.

"He could not get away with this in the States," I said. And that was true—I never saw a culture so much in love with babies and toddlers as the French. On the French highways, there were probably more ads with babies than with pretty women. The Michelin tire commercials with babies were quintessentially French. In the streets people stopped when they saw Joey, laughed, joked, teased him. A tired old man became happy looking at him, and wanted to touch his hair. "It's hot," Joey said. "It's burning." Joey had got burned on the iron once, and whenever we did not want him to touch something, we told him it was hot. Clearly, he understood our strategy. "Joey's hair is fire," he said.

Now, at the restaurant, we drank red wine, and ate our entrees: salmon, deer heart, lamb. When Joey was done with his highway, the waiters came, replaced the brown tablecloth with a white one, and brought Joey more chocolate. I ate some kind of cottage cheese mixed with sour cream, onions and bits of parsley. I enjoyed this, and this brought back memories of eating cottage cheese with onions in Croatia as a kid.

And that's where we would take Joey, to my hometown in Croatia to meet my mother, brother, and various relatives. On the way, we went to Rüschlikon, the suburbs of Zurich, where my brother and his wife studied theology at the Baptist Seminary. We drove into the mountains and went sledding with Joey. My brother and Joey went down the slopes, and Joey squealed, "Catch Ivo!" There were many people sliding down the slope. Ivo's kids, who spoke four languages, and in nightmares shouted in Swiss German, sledded as well.

In Zurich, since Joey loved trains, we took him into something similar, a tram. It was about eleven in the evening. Joey celebrated, stared out the glass into the streets at Christmas lights. People were entertained, but several of them angrily said, "Sleep, baby should sleep." Good thing we did not get arrested for abuse. Every baby should sleep by nine o'clock, or parents ought to be arrested. We all had jet lag; it was only five in the afternoon for us.

The next day we took a mountain train up Mt. Rigi. From there, on all sides we could see little towns, lakes, mountain peaks, as though we were looking on a picture map above which we hovered. Going down, we missed a train, and so we hiked. Each train station was about five minutes apart, and it took about fifteen minutes to walk the distance, going steeply downhill through evergreens, over streams, past castles. "That's where the green frog and the princess live," we told Joey, "in that castle." He pondered over that but did not say anything. I guess it puzzled him that something that seemed to be only in the picture book would also be out there in the real world, if he made such crass distinctions between the imagined world and the real world. At another stop we just missed the train. We sat in a train station the size of a shed, and listened to the creek below us rumbling and the wind being combed in the evergreen tree needles. I saw a little cart for carrying luggage, and said, "Let's put Joey on it and run down to the next station." We ran down the mountain path, skipped another train station, and kept running.

On the way to Croatia we visited Venice. It rained, so we bought a large umbrella, sipped cappuccinos, and walked, which proved hard, since Joey chased pigeons. He called them chicken. Generally, he knew how to distinguish fifty animals, but he did not make room for a distinction between chickens and pigeons. He jumped into puddles of water to splash it over the pigeons, and shrieked, "Fy chicken! Fy!"

Outside of Venice, at a rest area along the highway, we went to shop for wine and cheese to take to Croatia. When we got out, it was dark. We opened the car and drove, and it was only later, in Slovenia, that we discovered that the lock on one side was wrecked. Some Italian thieves broke into our car, probably with a screwdriver, and jacked the lock up. Breaking into locked cars is easy—I read that with a screwdriver it takes only about five seconds to break into most cars, Volvo about half a minute, Mercedes a minute and a half. What did the Italians steal? It turned out—a bag of diapers. We also had a suitcase with a thousand dollars in cash, but that one they left alone. And the camera was on the floor. It used to be in the diaper bag, but the thieves must have been in such a rush—maybe they saw us coming out of the store—that the camera fell back into the car. Now, I did not know that Italians wanted diapers this badly. This lowered my opinion of Italian organized crime, but maybe this was not organized. And later, when we went to buy diapers, we found out that it may not have been that unreasonable to steal them—they were three times more expensive than in the States, as was gasoline.

We had told Joey that he was an angel. And now when we took him to a castle in Slovenia, Mokrice, and showed him a sculpture of a winged angel, he said, "Mama, I have no wings." He pointed at his shoulders. He had discovered that he was not an angel, or that he was not a complete angel, and that hurt his feelings.

After Zagreb, we drove on the Highway of Brotherhood and Unity, the highway connecting Zagreb and Belgrade. Since the highway was blocked by two Serb enclaves, you could not go through to Belgrade, and the sign indicating directions said Lipovac, a village near the Serb border. We drove on a deserted highway, ninety miles an hour. There was very little light anywhere, and the asphalt was black. In a sixty-mile stretch we passed only four cars. We took the last exit before the Western Slavonian Serb enclave, and drove north, on country roads, toward Daruvar, my hometown. In the hills, it snowed and the roads were icy. At one point we saw fire, and I stopped. There were several soldiers standing around the fire, next to big piles of sandbags. Checkpoint. For a second I did not know whose it could be. Taking country roads, had we strayed to the enclave? These could be Serb soldiers, and it probably would not be healthy to get near them. But maybe it would be a Croatian checkpoint, and the Croats would turn us away and give us directions. But when we saw that one of the soldiers wore a white helmet, we realized that this was a UN checkpoint, and we drove on. The Nepali soldiers let us pass.

We arrived at my childhood home at three-thirty in the morning. The door was locked. I threw a stone up to the second floor, against the window pane, and pretty soon my mother peeked through.

Joey was ready to meet my mother, who was seventy-seven years old. We had prepared him for this by reading Strega Nona books. Strega Nona had a scarf on her head, a long nose, an apron, and wore clogs. "Joey, this is Strega Nona!" we said. He hid behind his mom, peeked over her ear, and clearly could not believe his luck. "Ah, so, that's the little blondie," my mother said, in Croatian. The Strega Nona book contained Italian words and Jeanette read it imitating the Italian accent, so this too must have made sense to him.

The following morning my mother prepared the dough, rolling and flattening it on the table, and then she cooked a dish of pasta with cabbage. Joey gazed at Strega Nona, pulled at her apron, kicked her clogs, pulled at her woolen socks, probably to test whether she was real.

Clogs may not seem like an important detail, but in this household they were. My parents used to make clogs, and my mother believed that the key to good health was having warm feet. Jeanette and Joey often walked barefoot. "How can they walk like that?" Mother asked me. "They'll get sick!"

She pointed at their feet, and said in English, "No! Shoes!" She knew about a hundred English words from having lived in Cleveland, Ohio until the age of three, and from watching American movies on TV. She raised her forefinger in a didactic manner.

And one night, Joey and Jeanette did get sick. First he got feverish and vomited, and then Jeanette did the same. Woken up by the noise and commotion at two in the morning, my mother came to our part of the house, and as soon as she saw Jeanette and Joey, who were right then vomiting into a tub, she said, "But they should have their boots on! I told you."

I said, "Look, they have some kind of stomach virus, you can't get that from bare feet."

"They should put their boots on right now."

"What are you? Mussolini's sister or something, to love boots so much?"

Fortunately, my older brother, who lived downstairs, was a doctor, and we called him. He gave Joey and Jeanette strong anti-bacterial medicine. They recovered in a day.

Though I ate the same things they did, I did not get sick, probably because I had grown up with the food bacteria. Jeanette thought this had to do with cheese, unpasteurized cottage cheese, similar to what I had eaten in the Parisian restaurant. She'd read something about it, and now thought that Joey could have died if he had not got the medicine in time. From now on, she was cautious with foods, but still walked barefoot around the apartment. Joey however, loved the new Italian leather boots we had bought for him on the way to Croatia, and you couldn't take them off him even in bed, unless he was asleep. He was proud of his boots, and his pride was augmented because wherever we went people laughed and said that the boots were beautiful. He probably believed my mother's word, that good boots guaranteed good health.

But although Jeanette was cautious with food, she was not cautious enough, according to my mother. Jeanette ate warm bread. That was one thing she had looked forward to—warm, tasty bread in the morning. But my mother had the theory that warm bread was bad for you, that it was sticky, and that it would tie your intestines into knots, and that you might die from it. My mother woke up every morning at six to buy bread and then stored it in the larder shelves. She hid fresh bread from us, and gave us bread that was at least three days old—now sufficiently dry to be good and safe. The problem was, it didn't taste so good any more. Peasants customarily baked their own bread once a week. On the sixth and the seventh day this theory—the older the bread, the healthier—served to keep kids from complaining, and my mother obviously believed what she'd grown up with. So we bought our own bread, and Jeanette hid it in a suitcase.

Mother also believed that you should never be exposed to a draught of air. No matter how hot it was in the room, she would not air it, and in that respect she was like most people in the Balkans, or at least in the former Yugoslavia. Once Jeanette and I traveled there on a bus, in the summer. Everybody sweated and panted, but nobody would open the windows, and when we tried, people shouted at us. In a train from Knin to Zadar, all the windows were closed, and the temperature must have been at least a hundred degrees. Jeanette opened the window, and one woman wept all the way. Jeanette thought that the woman wept because the window was open.

The main event for us, not for Joey, was our visit to the local Baptist church, a day before Christmas, for a blessing of children. Although the church had suffered schisms into the charismatic and non-charismatic branches, there were still almost as many people here as there were when I was a kid, about a hundred. Although the church was mostly Croatian, there were some Serbs in it, and the radical Croat nationalists in town dubbed the church the nest of Chetniks (Serb fascist royalists). Several Muslims attended the church as there was no mosque in town, and here they found the best reception, since the church's approach was multi-ethnic. After the lengthy sermon, the minister came to the front pew and talked in English to Jeanette and Joey, obviously proud of his linguistic skill. When the minister put his hands over Joey's head, Joey tried to kick him. "Go away, man, go away!" Joey shouted, just as the man was praying that Joey be given the gift of peace and love and tolerance. The man kept praying, and Joey, who was standing in front of him while Jeanette held him from behind, managed to deliver a good kick into the minister's shin. Here the Mussolini boots came in handy. The minister shrank back. Joey screamed, "Go away, man, go away!"

So the blessings were not long and it was doubtful how effective they could be. When I talked to my brother-in-law about this—an extremely pious Baptist, who had a fairly low opinion of the boastful minister—my brother-in-law laughed, and said, "You never know, sometimes even a rusty wire can conduct electricity."

Although I was skeptical about the business of blessings, I thought, Why not, it couldn't hurt, a quick dose of blessing, a quick fix that could send you off for a lifetime.

I won't discuss the long-term effects of blessings, but the short-term was not encouraging. During the Christmas Eve service, just as soulful melodies were sung pianissimo, Joey grabbed his mom's bra, pulling her breast into the strictly anti-nudity gathering. He shouted *Milka!*—not Milk but *Milka,* as though English were an inflected language. Jeanette was seated in the geographic middle of the church, in the aisle, since there were not enough seats. People fidgeted around uncomfortably. During the sermon, the minister talked the standard Christmas platitudes, peace on earth, etc., which of course, in the Balkans was not a platitude. He wished everybody peace, and even Joey, he mentioned, he wished him peace. And in his prayer, he said that people should discipline their children—it's never too early.

A church choir sang. Jeanette had taught Joey about angels, first in Notre Dame. He had been impressed by all kinds of toddlers, not much past the terrible twos, hovering above the dark candle-lit space, in stone, on their wings. He had seen more angels in a Catholic church in Switzerland. This church was all lit up, with fresh fresco colors and large stained windows through which sunlight and snowlight beamed, giving a light and airy Alpine sensation, while ruby-cheeked angels around the age of two floated. Jeanette now told Joey that the kids clad in white gowns were live angels. He was amazed, gazing intently, happy that another story turned out to be true. The story about winged toddlers who sang came to life here, and though they had no wings he believed that they were angels. After all, he was an angel and had no wings. Some of the kids looked scared; several kids seemed to be opening mouths without singing, as I used to when I was forced to sing in a chorus.

When the singing was over, before another round of prayers, Joey shouted, "Go home! Go home!" It wasn't clear to me whether he wanted the singers to go home, or us to go home, though most likely he wanted both. Of course, he could have shouted something worse, as he did in the Baptist church in Rüschlikon, Zurich, his first church attendance ever, during the quietest moment of prayer: "Poopy diapers! Poopy diapers!" Maybe he would have shouted that too, if he had not lost all sense of patience and optimism: he screamed, kicked, spat like a tomcat.

And so Jeanette, Joey, and I walked out of the overheated church. No, we did not mind this. He freed us.

RUTH'S DEATH

IT'S HARD FOR ME to write about parents since I know more about children than about parents. That is because when I was a child, I was more interested in myself and my siblings than in my parents, and now that I am a parent, I find our children more interesting than us. I remember my parents saying I would understand what they said when I grew older. I still don't understand them. My father died when I was eleven and I was a bit estranged from my mother because Father and Mother made a simple game—I was his favorite, and my older brother Ivo was hers. She was still alive, eighty-seven, when I wrote these lines, and now that she has died I am rewriting.

She had been ill for five years. We expected her to die after her heart attack, stroke, diagnosis with diabetes, food poisoning, and herpes shingles which gave her chronic neuralgia. Jeanette, our two children, and I went to Daruvar for her birthday party, May 27. Her middle name was May; she was born in the States, in Cuyahoga County, before the river went up in flames and before the world did too, in 1918, one month before the Sarajevo assassination.

She was paler than usual; her hair, which had stayed half black until her eightieth birthday, was now completely white, her green-hazel eyes seemed to have grown smaller although they had always been small, under high-arched eyebrows, and she looked startled, caught in a role she didn't like. She had seemed to be the strong one, taking care of the others who were sick, and this change surprised her.

As we slurped tomato soup my daughter Eva, who was three years old at the time, asked, Are you a ghost?

Mother, who could understand some English, wanted us to translate. (She could sing *Mary had a little lamb* before her final illness).

I said, I am not sure I should translate.

Why not? She looked like a turtle, with all the creases and ancient caution, as though I could harm her.

Well, she asks whether you are a ghost. It's quaint how a child sees things.

My mother didn't seem to find it quaint. She didn't laugh, didn't comment. She gave me a look with her shrinking head, and I felt put in my place in this biology of life and death. Who the hell was I to tell her about life and death? Mothers took care of survival.

I felt I needed to explain more, and I said, See, we told her that you were gravely ill and that we should rush to see you before you die.

So, when will she become a spirit? asked my daughter. I am the first person in the world Eva saw, as my wife had a C-section, and I think that she still trusts me in the primary-imprinting kind of way.

What did she ask now? Mom asked.

I translated again. Eva had her own theology, that everybody dies but first becomes a ghost, and gradually, when the ghost learns how to fly very well, it quits hanging around the body, dies for the second time, and goes into the heavens.And when it has nothing more to do with the body, it is a spirit, a spirit in the sky.

Your grandma is fully alive, I said to Eva. She's just pale; that doesn't mean she's a ghost.

But I wanted to see a ghost. I've never seen one.

We slurped our tomato soup in silence, and Eva kept glancing up at her grandmother and grandmother at Eva. Mother had wanted us to name Eva Ruth. None of her grandchildren or great-grandchildren had the name Ruth, and she wondered why. I said that names sound better when they end in a vowel, which you can enjoy in your vocal cords for a long while.

I used to be Ruta for many years, she said, until you all got hold of my birth certificate and saw that I was named Ruth, so I started using my original name. You could have called someone Ruta in Croatian.

Sure, but it sounds like the road. Who wants to be trampled on? I asked, and thought, Holy cow, what a question. Wasn't she trampled on, like a route?

We visited Ruth several times, always expecting her to die shortly afterward. Once, after her collapse consisting of a heart attack and stroke, we came to Pakrac Hospital, where she lay in a ward. We drove in an old Volkswagen Bug borrowed from a friend. It was winter and the windows couldn't be completely closed and the heat didn't work. We were freezing during the two-hour trip through side-roads and damaged villages. Many houses were burned down, but as they were made of stone and brick they still stood. Some floors and roofs had collapsed from the beams' burnout. Many houses had bullet holes in the mortar. We passed through two deserted villages on the way, with thin snow sporadically covering the ground. The hospital itself was mostly destroyed, with howitzer and anti-aircraft bullet holes in the gray walls. My older brother Vlado used to work in this hospital as an ophthalmologist. Now he worked independently, but he still knew the cardiologist who had remained in the hospital. Vlado claimed that the first missile of the Yugoslav war landed in his bed at the hospital. The Yugoslav army surrounded Pakrac and started shelling the hospital under the pretext that there were Croatian policemen there. A missile went through the window and landed on the bed. As the bed was soft and the bomb required a strong impact to go off, it didn't explode. My brother was supposed to be there that night and he would have been probably in bed that early in the morning. He had stayed home to pay attention to his sick wife, a woman whose family was obliterated by the Serbian *chetniks* in the Second World War, in front of her eyes, and who, despite her initial good looks, retained a sorrowful face.

On the way to the hospital, on the former highway of Bratsva i jedinstva (Brotherhood and Unity) we saw bunnies. A large brown hawk sat on a walnut tree. In the hospital yard, crows hopped among chickens. We walked in and asked to see Ruth Novakovic. Kindly nurses led us there. Ruth was sharing a room with two other elderly women. She sat up when she saw us. How are you? I asked.

How could I be? *Svakako.* Any which way. Bad and good.

It's all right here in the hospital?

Yes, we talk and talk. What else can we do?

We know everything about your children, said a woman in the bed next to hers.

And I know everything about her extended family. It's like a conference of biographers here, my mother said. All that remains after so many of us is stories.

Good that you can remember so many lives, I said. I would make a terribly boring patient. I'd have to resort to telling jokes.

That would be sad, Mom said. There's more to life than ridicule.

We wanted our son to play the cello for her.

He doesn't have to play for me, she said.

He will anyway, I replied. It was a small cello and he made a beautiful sight and sound, so little as he was with the little cello, with long blond hair, stringing out various etudes.

How do you like his playing? I asked.

I am not an expert. I don't understand any of it.

You don't have to understand it—do you enjoy listening to him?

I am too busy thinking about it all, all of you, so many people, to talk about pleasure now.

I remembered now. It was hard to get a compliment out of my mother, and I was fishing for one, obviously. If it never worked for me, maybe it should work for my son. Not that I needed a compliment for me, but I wanted one for my son's well being and my mother's well being, a moment of satisfaction, an insight that life has been good after all because, look at it, the offspring is talented and beautiful. Maybe there was such a moment of satisfaction in her as she listened and breathed heavily. She simply didn't have the means of expressing that satisfaction verbally and habits dominated the patterns of speech, especially now—what is the right thing to say as someone seems to be deathly ill? We all floundered; customs didn't seem to provide the necessary ammunition. Ammunition to kill the awkwardness?

But her thinking also couldn't be changed. How much does the cello cost? she asked. How can you pay for all of that? Isn't that reckless of you?

Yes, it is reckless, I said. And it would also be reckless not to spend anything on the cello and children's music education. Remember how our father tried to turn us into musicians, how he bought a piano, and then an organ, and a violin, and none of us would play, but here, don't you think he would be delighted if he saw his grandson, if he could see him?

Yes, he would be, she said. He was wild about music. But he was not a realist.

But don't you love music?

Oh, don't worry about what I think.

Well, we don't need to quarrel as there's nothing to quarrel about, I said. Some things are good, and you see we are proud of him.

Poor kid. Do you feed him enough?

Yes, we do our best.

He should have a little more color in his cheeks.

He'll get it in the summer.

But where will you be in the summer? I hope not in Russia again.

In Russia, after all, I said. They have more sunshine there than anybody in the summer—white nights.

Oh yes, then you won't be able to sleep.

You've never been much of a sleeper yourself, I said.

No, I had to worry about everything all the time, and now it doesn't matter. If I had known it would all end up like this, I would have slept more. But even that doesn't matter now. It really is all the same.

That's a relaxing thought, isn't it?

I wish I could just fall asleep and never wake up. Being dead would be better than this.

How can you say that?

You have no idea how much pain I have.

From the heart attack?

No, that hasn't bothered me that much. But these nerves on my left side and my back, they feel like I am on fire. That never goes away, no pain killers, nothing helps, and it just grinds me down.

That does sound terrible.

I don't know how that happened. And my brother has the same neurological illness except it attacked his eyes, and he is blind, and he says he feels like scratching his eyes out of his sockets, his eyes itch and hurt so much.

I know, I visited him. At least he follows all the news and discusses politics, more than when he was healthy.

Yes, when he was healthy, he was drunk. I think he was drunk for thirty years, so you couldn't hear any smart idea from him then, and he slurred so badly I couldn't understand what he was saying and when I did, it wasn't worth the effort. I am surprised that he can make so much sense now, that his brain is so good. He sounds like a president.

That's not much of a compliment. Well, for someone who's had a heart attack and a stroke, you seem to be totally alert.

The pain keeps me alert.

Maybe pain is good for you after all.

It can't be.

She had other crises, and we rushed to see her and gathered around her, and no longer talked about ghosts. The last time I visited her—I visited six times in three weeks but could never stay for longer than an hour as she would get exhausted— she expressed her love of animals. She always enjoyed cats but didn't ask for one. Vlado, who lived downstairs from her, and took care of her, has a large dog, but no cats, and his wife hated cats.

I heard there's a family of hedgehogs living in the bushes downstairs, she said. One of them caught a birdie which fell out of a nest, a little swallow, and carried it to their lair. It was all naked and hairless, and when Vlado prodded the hedgehog with a stick, it still wouldn't let go of the birdie but ran with it to the other hedgehogs.

That's kind of nice, I said, although it sounded terrible as well.

Maybe it fed its young ones like that.

It's possible. Have you seen them? Would you like to see them?

I probably would but I don't need to. Life like that is interesting. I've seen a lot of life. You know, we lived in the village, where my misguided dad ran a farm, if you could call it that. What a failure he was! But he loved animals, you know. He had many good moments with cows, dogs, cats, goats, geese, donkeys, doves. He loved doves, and his grandson, Pepik, inherited that disease. He had a collection of carriers. Poor boy!

True, my cousin was devoted to letter-carrier pigeons. And this kind of love of animal life was part of our extended family. Just knowing that there was such life around her seemed to comfort her. There she was similar to my daughter, who loves animals so much that we have several anecdotes. One: Eva picked up a snake. The snake bit her. Eva cried. Why are you crying? Jeanette asked. Because my snake left me. She slipped into the bushes and I can't find her anymore.

I wrote this section while Ruth was still alive, and that's why it's in the present tense, in parts. Mom sits in a house where I grew up, and stays in the room where my father died. It used to be Mose Pijade 43, named after a communist, Tito's adviser in World War II. Now it's named Jelacica 43, after a Croatian governor who helped suppress the Hungarian National Revolt in 1948. It's a big house, which took many years to build, made of stone and brick, very solid, although in my dreams the house is falling apart, with the walls swelling, moving, warping.

When I visit her I can't stay very long. She keeps her windows closed, all but one, because she is scared of draughts. There's a musty smell there. Since she can't walk to the bathroom, she keeps her large potty right there, and my brother empties it every evening when he comes to make sure she has taken all her pills. That's the smell of old age, then. In the States, she would be in an old people's home, and perhaps that would be better, but here my brother takes care of her, and he considers that superior to the alienation of old age. She doesn't need much company and she is among her own, Vlado says, and talks: I know Czechs in this area, who, as soon as their parents are over seventy, no matter what shape they are in, ship them into nursing homes or put them in far-away villages to die alone, like sick cats. That is shameful. I had a patient here, an old Czech, and her son kept asking how long she had to live yet, and was disappointed, clearly, when I said she could live ten years. In all that, my brother may have forgotten that we are quarter Czechs ourselves. He is not eager to see Czechs in a good light, apparently. At the same time, it's pretty heroic of him to be taking care of her for years now. His vacations are limited by whether he can find care for her—and now that he is at the coast, he has a sturdy woman in her mid-forties helping out. She is a housekeeper for the old castle in the middle of the park, which used to be the school where I finished my elementary education; and now it is partly a museum and to a large extent, a wine-cellar. Well, it always had fine cellars from which the smell of old oak, soaked in wine and rotting slowly, for decades, spread and wafted up the corridors into our classroom. No wonder so many of my classmates became alcoholics, and at least two of them, out of thirty, have already died from alcoholism. That woman now cleans the museum and castle, living with her two sons, without a husband. I met her, and she talked eagerly and loudly, but was clearly good natured, an old style peasant. She comes in three times a day now and delivers the food. My mother eats minimally, half a potato a day, a slice of bread with honey, a glass of milk, a slice of orange. She doesn't move much but keeps listening and looking. She is a bit deaf, so her TV set is loud. She used to be a big reader. In a way she represents the history of culture here and abroad—the defeat of the written word. When I borrowed books from the library, such as the *Village of Stepanichkovo* by Dostoyevski, she would rebuke me for reading too much and then even before I'd get to read the book, she would finish it, and would comment on what a waste of time it was.

A cousin of mine, who didn't like to read much, had respect for Ruth, and she asked her for advice, What novel should I read? I am on vacation.

Tess by Hardy is excellent, Ruth said, and the cousin read the book and loved it.

When did you read the novel? I asked her.

Years ago, when my mother and I lived in Zagreb. Mother had divorced Papa, and she took me along to Zagreb, while my little brothers stayed with the stepmother, who, by the way, was an angel. She never had a child of her own, and she had to put up with Papa's pining after my mother. Once a week or so he'd go into a diatribe about how much he missed her, and what a mistake it was that he let her go, and Strina, his new wife, never objected to it, but loved him till death.

So where did you live in Zagreb?

Where? What could we do? Mother worked as a nanny for a German-Jewish family who owned a textile factory near the center. They liked the idea of raising their children bilingual, and they paid Mary pretty well because of her English. I helped in the house with the dishes, cleaning, and babysitting. They had a fine library and I read in my spare time, and Tess was my favorite.

How long did you stay there?

Not long, just a couple of years. When I got married, I went back to the village, but Mary stayed. When the king of Yugoslavia signed the pact with Hitler, the family talked about leaving, to America, and they offered to take even me along. Your dad had already been in the army for two years but he wasn't coming home.

The Germans overran Yugoslavia, and the gendarmes came to the house and took the family away to the train station, for Poland. They kicked us out into the streets.

What happened to the family?

You know what happened. You know what the beasts did with the Jews. Tears rolled down her cheeks, but she composed herself and went on.

Mary volunteered to join the partisans. She hated the Germans and their Ustasha helpers who kicked her new family out of the house. She wanted a gun, but there weren't enough guns then, and so she worked as a nurse till the end of the war, and when Tito came to Zagreb near the end, she was his nurse.

Wow, she had quite a lot of adventures, then, I said. Strange, she never spoke to me about any of it in Cleveland, but read hundreds of war novels. She could never have enough of war in her head. And you never talked about it. How come I never heard about this period of your life?

Why would you? You never asked, and you never listened.

Is that where you learned to speak German? Or was it Yiddish? You always seemed to have a strange vocabulary, with words from all over.

Earlier on I stayed with the Brkic family, Ruth went on, and they spoke mostly German at home. Anyway, I think those years in Zagreb were the happiest years in Mom's life, strangely enough.

She enjoyed hanging out with guys, that's true, I said. When I visited her in Cleveland (where she returned several years after the war), and when she was old and frail, she would limp to the fire-station a block away, and hang out with the firefighters. She talked to them, and they listened, and laughed, and said to me, Your Grandma is a hoot! But she wasn't a hoot with me, she told me nothing. But then you don't tell me everything either. How come I never knew you lived in Zagreb? You could tell me more about the war, I am sure.

I could, I am sure, but I am too tired now.

Anyway, a year later, I bought a ticket to see her after my classes at Penn State ended. She seemed to be able to last, but I heard that she couldn't get out of bed and that boded no good. I was sitting in the lobby of Juilliard, where my son was spending the day taking classes and participating in the chamber and orchestral activities, and since I had seven hours free, I was making phone calls to see whether any of my friends were free to get together for coffee or a stroll in the park. In the middle of my leaving a message, there was beep, someone trying to call me, and it was my brother from Minneapolis. Vlado called, he said. Mother died this morning.

It was not unexpected but it was not expected either. Still a shock.

Any details? How did she die? What about the funeral? (That felt now like chatter. Nothing changes Mom's death.)

Apparently, she was a bit better than a few days ago, and even had a meal, kasha or something, and later when Vlado came back to give her medication, she was dead. He thinks she simply fell asleep.

She didn't want to live any more, I said.

Yes, for a long time she claimed it, but she must have really grown tired of being in bed and not being able to sit up.

Will you go to the funeral?

I don't know—we'll look for tickets, but last minute, it's hard, and they aren't going to wait for us. They will bury her in three days. In this country, it can be delayed, but there, they don't do that, they don't refrigerate the dead.

No yet, anyway.

Oh, shit, what to do? To pull out my son from his classes, and fly? But I hate funerals, they are either morbid and depressing, or duplicitously uplifting. I had just been to a memorial which was presented as the happiest occasion on earth, with lots of smiles and laughs, and I didn't believe the mood. It was a Prozac memorial. Well, maybe it wasn't, maybe the spirit was really so uplifting.

I walked around the block of gray concrete, NY Public Library, Lincoln Center, Tower Records. . . nothing Ruth would identify as home. To begin with, this was the center of New York. She was Cleveland steel trash, fodder for the industry and economy there. I walked and I was dizzy. My step was not steady; although I had rehearsed in my mind the moment of walking at my mother's funeral, the rehearsal didn't help; it would be a cliché to have a crisis of nerves now. When someone dies, how original can you be? Ignore the death? Indulge it by losing it? What the hell can I do? I know, this is all normal. We will all die and it will be all normal. This is the illness for which there is no help. Religion? Should I pray now? I spent half of my youth in religious frenzy, but where is it now? I got it all wrong—it would have been better to be an indifferent agnostic in youth, and religious in old age, just as it would be better to be sober until old age and then to drink. No, I am not going to pray. It would be an opportunistic moment. Maybe I will pray in a month. Maybe I will gather enough faith for that. Now I am just plain ill.

I went out and re-parked the car from the metered slot into a yard, and I sat there, and didn't feel like getting out of it. I called up my wife, to see whether she could dig up some cheap last-minute fares to Croatia. She didn't think I should go— maybe it would be better to have a memorial service sometime in December and we could all gather then?

The cheapest ticket at first was $2400 for flying out the same day. Yes, one shouldn't think of money in a moment like this, but in addition to everything else, this would be a financial blow. In many American and other-national "good families," people grieve and then inherit a chunk of property. A friend of mine from California bought a huge house in England; his mother died, and now he's happy, and just got married in his new spacious home. In a way, he made out. My brother would inherit the section of home where Mother lived, but he had earned it tenfold—nothing could repay him the ten years of constant care in his best years. I wasn't thinking of all that at that moment in New York as I walked aimlessly, but I did want to get a cheap airfare to Croatia, not to end up bankrupt as well as grieving.

We had recently gone to Jeanette's father's burial, and then we all drove, the whole family, the four of us, to Nebraska. It was winter, a cold day. Her father had frozen to death. He had insisted on taking a drive with his wife on the coldest day in December, to look at the pastures where he used to have a herd of cattle. The cattle had grazed for forty years with his help; he left mineral supplements for them in the fields, large blocks of salted stuff which the cows loved to lick, and I helped him with that. Somehow, he never had a four-wheel drive, and he managed to navigate through mud and snow in the hills with his Toyota pick-ups. This time he got stuck in a snowdrift, and his wife went to town to get someone to pull them out, and by the time she got back, Ken was dead.

I had received the news; Jeanette's mother had called, Ken passed away. How and when, I asked, and she told me the story. I called Jeanette at her work, and said, Your father died. (I never liked the expression passed away, or the recently fashionable, passed. . . Death can't be softened). She broke into tears and rushed home. I canceled my flight to Colorado College and we drove. When we got to Creighton, Jeanette wanted to drive by the morgue, and there in the window, she saw the sign, Kenneth Baldwin. Up till then we had kept up a reasonably cheerful conversation, even occasionally praising the fullness of life Ken had had, doing all he had dreamed of, even visiting Croatia and Greece, and Alaska and Mexico. As a self-made cowboy, he tended westward more than eastward, and I was seen by the cowboy family, when we lived in Nebraska, as an alien element, and I never seemed to fit in, which didn't bother me, nor them—they liked it that way: Europeans, stay away. Anyway, Jeanette broke down when she saw the sign late at night after the long trip. We drove through the little part of Creighton, Nebraska, with all of its holiday exhibits—elves working, Santa riding through the snow, happy sights for children—but death made it all appear mechanical and hollow.

Oh, but it is not this death that I am writing about, deserving though it is of particular attention, as my mother's death. I wondered, why should I take my mother's death more stoically than Jeanette took her father's? What is it? Was I trained like that? I knew that Mother would want me to take it stoically, the way she took her husband's death—even though for years she kept visiting his grave and leaving flowers there. I suppose I was trained—tragedy was the norm, and when I was a kid, after my father died, two of his brothers did, and many other relatives, and I quit going to funerals. There were wars, there were all sorts of repressive governments, there was inevitable misery, that was the family ethos, and to top that, we were Baptists, so death was a challenge to be overcome. *Death, where is thy sting?* was the motto. We would transcend death through faith. Anyhow, she is dead, so how I react makes no difference to her. It won't get her to heaven, it won't bring her back to life. It's only for me, how I would feel now. I feel terrible, and I don't need to feel better at the moment. Well, I don't need to deceive myself. For years I was getting used to the idea of the entropy of her life—she could do less and less, her valves were gone more and more after several heart attacks, her muscles could do less and less, and finally I couldn't even call her. She was there, but she had no strength to pick up the phone.

Once the phone fell from her hands and she didn't pick it up again.

On her eighty-eighth birthday, as most of us tried to call her, she didn't answer the phone. After the first attempt to get to the phone, she fell on the floor, and later she fell again, and had to go to the hospital with a concussion.

And yet somehow she still stayed alive, and the family enjoyed the idea that everything else was failing but her brain was lucid and intact.

But while I was in Russia after her birthday, Vlado reported that her brain in the CAT-scan showed signs of shrinking.

I was stuck with a strange visa, so I couldn't leave Russia for a month, and by then she was better, but not well enough to take a longer visit, and my brother Vlado was not encouraging it. It would stress her out. She needs calm.

But what does she need it for?

To get better.

Does she want to get better?

I work on the assumption that she does; I can't work on another assumption. I can only help her live, not help her die. I am not Dutch. They believe in euthanasia. For my part, I believe there is no good death. No matter how it takes place, it is miserable. I want to help her live as long as possible.

That is admirable, but still, perhaps she would like to see everybody and then die?

I imagine if she saw everybody, she would die from exhaustion. But you've been here several times to see her, I don't think you need to come again.

And so I didn't. I did think she couldn't last, so I bought a ticket to see her in December, after my classes. I thought she could hang in, she had hung in for so long.

Later, when Ivo and I talked about her life, we rationalized a little, not necessarily excusing our not visiting more. She was not into celebration. If you came there, she would wonder how much money you had spent, and she would regret such unreasonable living. Couldn't you save that money? Don't you think you should buy some property? How will you live in old age if you have nothing? Why keep traveling? What's the point?

Well, I came to see you.

That sounds fine, but we can talk on the phone and you can send me pictures.

True enough, she had pictures of the whole family on the cupboard, and she loved getting those, and she spent a lot of time looking at them, and if she had a visitor, when she was still hale, she'd show the pictures and explain who was who. And she could keep the extended family tree all intact in her head, better than anybody, without ever writing anything down.

But she seemed to treasure visits indirectly, and to talk about them years later. However, at the moment of the visit, she expressed only skepticism, and then, criticism:why are you so thin (or fat), why don't you exercise more, why don't you take better care of yourself, do you need to drink at all, and why don't you go to church, it's a shame, all your ancestors were such believers, and you are going to quit that tradition? What gives you the right? And so on. I found it hard to take the criticism, although I should have taken it in stride as a way of talking, not ill meant. And maybe there was some wisdom in the remarks. Not that I would change, but yes, that was the point, somehow she always wanted the change, for the better to her mind.

She never wanted to praise. She didn't praise my son, and she never praised me for publishing my books. In fact, she didn't read them. They were in English, after all, and by the time they were translated, she could no longer see well enough, but she also didn't want to have them read to her as she didn't have much faith in what I'd say. It would have been far better if he hadn't dropped out of med school, she said. It looked like he would become a reasonable and productive person, and then he dropped out and went into this fantasy world, which does nobody any good. Nobody reads anymore and nobody needs to, so why are you writing? You can only disgrace the family like that, with some *psine*. In Croatian, that literally means *nasty dog play*.

One theory I heard in the family about why she never wanted to praise is this. After having a son and daughter who lived, and before having the younger set (three of us, my sister Nela, Ivo, and me), she gave birth to two daughters, who died, one at the age of one, and the other at the age of four. They were supposedly both beautiful, especially so the four year old, Ljerka. One day, Mother had visitors, and she said to them, Look how beautiful and how smart she is. She can already add numbers.

And people looked at her and said, You are right, she is beautiful and smart, an extraordinary child. She will have a great future.

But soon after the guests left, Ljerka turned blue from meningitis, and died.

That was a big blow. Out of four children, two died.

My father's brother, Pero, named his daughter Ljerka, to comfort his brother, and to say, life goes on. There's a beautiful and smart daughter.

So, when we were born, Mom didn't praise us, and she made it a scrupulous principle not to boast of her children. She would be proud, but would keep it to herself. Sometimes her eyes would flicker knowingly, but perhaps she was afraid to acknowledge it.

Instead, she criticized, especially so with me because she actually had a good reason to be critical. She would scrutinize me skeptically ever since I had TB at the age of six. I suppose to her mind I was a goner then. I was thin, tall for my age, and I spent a year in fevers and coughs. I pulled through it and became a strong kid, jumping from trees, wrestling with boys my age and winning. But she didn't like that, either. I was wild. And then every winter I had bronchitis, sort of a bad habit of my lungs, and coughed mercilessly for months at a time, trying to suppress the cough in the down pillows, and when I slept, I sweated and drooled. If I coughed at night, she would turn the lights on and look at me with displeasure and sorrow. Why don't you cover yourself better? Why did you walk barefoot? Why don't you take more syrup? Why won't you drink chamomile? Somehow she could impart it to me that it was my fault, a moral failing, that I was afflicted with various childhood diseases. I was a good student, but she didn't expect that to last, and it didn't. This skepticism was also the way she treated my father, who, when partisan officers came over to her place when she lived in a miserable basement, and said, Your husband is now a communist fighter, you deserve better quarters, she replied, Oh, is he now? He left his old army? You know, it may not last. Knowing him, I think he'll give up your army too. And she refused to get a three-bedroom apartment from them as she couldn't trust the change of fortunes.

She didn't want much, and she didn't expect much. It was maddening for me that she expected so little and that she worked so hard.

When my father died, she took over the business of making wooden clogs, and worked day in and day out, and she also gardened, raising all sorts of produce, and she cleaned the Baptist church, took care of several old and sick women for free, cooked for us, woke up early to put wood in the stoves, and so on.

The strange thing is that she died in the same room in which her husband had died thirty-nine years before. She did not remarry and she stayed faithful to his memory. I don't know why, whether she was tempted to remarry or not, whether she thought it would be a disgrace to do it, but she stayed alone from the age of forty-nine, which is very young. After all, I am fifty as I write this.

From my childhood, I considered the bedroom of our parents a secret chamber I wasn't allowed to visit without knocking, a terrifying chamber. And it became even more terrifying after witnessing Father's death there. I never wanted to sleep in the room where he died. She had a choice of that room or another, brighter and bigger, but she chose that one, and that is where she slept for all those years, and where she was bedridden for the last two, and where she died. To my mind, that is amazing, to die in the same room. I mean, I am now in a plane going to Budapest, and then, on to Daruvar by car or train, for the funeral, but anyhow, I am on the go. I have no idea where I will die, where I will live. I may be buried, and probably will be, in the same cemetery where most of my ancestors are buried, in Daruvar, if there's enough money and time and refrigeration to transport me back there, but I am not going to speculate on that, and I could end up elsewhere, which would be just fine with me. I am not that faithful to one location. There's clearly pressure to be location-faithful. In my stories, I have written too much about Croatia and Yugoslavia. . . Maybe it's enough to have a mental faithfulness to the place. But there are other places now, where I have lived, where I have experienced, where I want to live.

The plane is not all that full. I asked for the exit row for the leg space on Delta, and I got two seats all to myself. The stewardesses are polite and my neighbors are tired. It reminds me of traveling to Europe after 9/11, when there was plenty of space on the planes but also an aura of suspicion and depression. I don't know what it will be like to see my aging siblings. I am the youngest one. You can get to be the youngest one at the age of fifty. In some countries, it's over the average life expectancy. My father died at the age of fifty-three. In Russia, the average death age for men is fifty-seven. Maybe it's up to fifty-nine, now that nearly all the severe alcoholics who were tempted to die from too much drinking already did so.

My oldest sister Nada is an old woman at the age of seventy. She has all sorts of twitches and she never recovered fully from the recent wars.

It is easy to canonize one's parents, especially mothers. Fathers, it's easy to demonize them. But I was not the only one doing that. I remember a cousin of mine, who gave me a sermon about what a saint my mother was. She had taken care of his blind mother for years, taken her out for walks, visiting her for conversation. That old woman, Marica, is dead by now. Most everybody among Ruth's friends is dead. That happens when you are eighty-eight.

Nearly the entire family gathered at my brother's house, which for his wife was stressful. She has gone through chemotherapy and radiation, and now is undergoing another round of chemotherapy and very weak, so, it's no wonder that for half an hour she hid in her bedroom. She had taken care of my mother as much as anybody else. When I sat with her alone before the party, while Vlado still worked, helping the nearly blind, she wept. I said the worst was over, no more suffering.

I don't see it that way, she said.

It's a relief for Vlado and you not to have to toil for her.

That is not much of a consolation. The house will be frightfully empty, she said.

You could have renters.

No, it's not the same.

I took a whole week off from work, and I wasn't taking care of the funeral details, unlike Vlado, who worked even on the day of the funeral, a couple of severe cases. He said he didn't know all the details that had to be taken care of, such as *smrtovnica*, the black-edged paper announcing her death to townspeople and listing all the grieving relatives, the closest ones, such as siblings, and direct descendants and their spouses, but not cousins and the extended family. There were thirty-eight listed, and he worried that he would misspell some foreign names, which he did. Casket to order, corpse to be taken to the morgue. Now that is a big change from the way it was done in my childhood. Then, the corpse would be laid out in state, usually in the living room and sometimes in the bedroom. A black flag was posted on the house, and friends and relatives came and visited and paid homage at home, and the relatives sometimes slept even in the same room as the corpse. When my father died, he stayed in the living room, to my horror, and I felt a terrible relief when he was taken out and put in the ground...of course, more horror. Now, she wasn't there in the house. Her smell in the room where she lived for the last twenty years stayed there. It was on the second floor, which may have speeded up her demise. If she had stayed on the ground floor, she would have been able to move, to walk, to keep her body functioning a little longer. It is hard to say what got her, but from food poisoning, she also had a heart attack, and so on, an entire list of illnesses.

It was great to see some thirty relatives gathered there. Some of them were young, and looked good, dressed formally in black, and it seemed a shame we had never gathered like that while Ruth was alive, other than for my father's funeral, when half of these people weren't born yet. It would have cheered her up, no doubt, to see them all gathered. And it was a shame we couldn't take a picture to show her. She enjoyed looking at pictures of relatives.

Suddenly we all had reason to think about health. A neighbor across the road from us, it turned out, was dying during that time.

It was a sunny and blue day. Vlado was the only one who did not have a black suit but a dark blue one. I said, don't worry, blue counts as a color of grief, that's what the blues is called after. 9/11 was a blue day.

OK, I'll take that, he said.

Unlike in the old-style burials with horse-drawn carriages, after which we walked through the entire town, stopping traffic, this one was localized to the cemetery. We parked the cars outside the cemetery. Some of us walked to it, and then gathered around the morgue, and formed a procession which went around the cemetery. Not much time to walk and think. We the siblings, five of us, gathered before and went in to the morgue to examine the wreaths with our names inscribed. I hadn't even read what mine said, I couldn't find it, but I trusted Vlado that it was there and that the appropriate words were on it.

In the coffin, she looked like a classic grandmother, with a shawl around her head, her cheeks sunken, nose prominent, thin, hooked, and her hands large and knotty, almost larger than her head, which had somewhat shrunken with age. Her hands were pale, almost white, off-white. Mother's hands were almost as large as her head in the casket. When I looked at her, I wondered why not have *Totenhaende*, death hands imprinted in plaster, to last forever? I had seen only two death masks, as a pretentious tourist, Beethoven's and Liszt's. Her eyes, also sunken, were much smaller than when she was younger. There was no spasm on her face, which my brother claimed indicated that she did not die in pain. She had fallen asleep. Her nerves failing before her death might have helped obliterate the pain of dying.

I touched her forehead. The skin and the underlying flesh were cold and spongy, thicker than I had expected. Vlado said when he had found her dead she had already lost two degrees Celsius, which indicated she had been dead for two hours as one loses one degree per hour. I am not sure what temperature she was at now, but she was very cold.

Yes, peaceful was good, but peaceful and warm are synonymous when it comes to life, not peaceful and cold.

Relatives came and shook hands, kissed cheeks, expressed condolences. Glassy and shiny-eyed, we kept our composure, and perhaps it would have been more difficult if the death had been sudden and if there had not been the consolation of the end of the suffering. Postponing the death would have led nowhere as she definitely couldn't get out of bed again.

The two women who took care of her when she couldn't get out of bed, feeding her, changing her, washing her, and massaging, they both wept, and talked to her. I had seen that before, people trying to talk to the dead in the casket—and it was touching. It was good to know that the people who had known Ruth best in her last days loved her. Often it happens that the old become unbearable and outright nasty and their caretakers grow to resent them, but the attachment and love which these women obviously had for her was good, at least for me, to contemplate. Therefore, I was surprised when I found out that Vlado had not invited them to the dinner memorial party afterward at a restaurant near the park.

After a sermon that didn't do much for me, a choir sang, and even though the singing was amateurish, it was effective in inducing sorrow. I had heard it at other funerals in my youth. *Zbogom.* Literally, *With God,* which is used as a greeting when someone leaves for a long time. I couldn't control my chin when I listened to the song. It twitched.

The morticians, four of them, pushed the cart with rubber wheels along the cemetery and up the hill.

The grave was dug shallow, to place her casket above my father's. It was about five feet, less. The soil dug out was clay, mostly greenish brown, without many stones. After another sermon and singing, I looked at the gravepit. Yes, dust to dust. There were many flowers all around, and bees landed on them and collected pollen. Death, where is thy sting? Bees, yes, there should be bees at this funeral. My father had been a bee-keeper, one of my sisters, Nada, is a bee-keeper, my father's *smrtovnica* had the motto, Death, where is thy sting? The bees liked this death. They would sting if I tried to touch them.

The minister, who had spent ten years in Australia and had been a baker before, turned the eulogy into a sermon, as could be expected, inviting people to accept Jesus as their personal savior in order to die well, rather, to live eternally. I remembered that when my father died, another minister took it as an opportunity for a sales pitch—a perfect death, such as everybody should desire, thanks to God. But, let him do his thing, I thought. My mother, who was a firm believer all her life, would have understood this, would have perhaps even liked this invitation to faith. She had been a shy woman all her life, she wouldn't have liked this much attention anyway, and the speech turning away from her to divine matters would please her.

Vlado thanked the people for coming to the funeral, while holding on to the gravestone with the names of his father, mother, sisters. Maybe he needed to hold on, maybe he was unsteady, but merging with the stone, he was steady, the backbone of the funeral. Mother had her name inscribed a month after Father's funeral, with her birth year, 1918, and then the year of death uncut. It still had to be cut into the stone, 2006.

Vlado was the first to throw in a fistful of soil, and it thudded on the wood softly. Ivo picked up a fistful from the same heap and a soft thud followed. I suppose I wanted to be a bit less imitative, so I picked up a chunk of soil as large as my fist from the far left and dropped it after looking down into the pit. The sound that came out surprised me. It was sharp, loud—I had thrown a stone coated in soil. This was an aggressive sound of stone-throwing. I recoiled from that. That is not what I had intended. The other siblings threw in the soil and some grandchildren did. So I threw a stone at her casket, unknowingly. Does that symbolize what kind of son I was? I wondered.

There was no sensation of relief once it was all done. It's all done, the suffering is over, she is in a better world, I felt none of that. Death, where is thy sting—it would be good to know where exactly, but this sting is diffuse, in the veins, arteries, general blue tone of the day. Perfect day. We all got a suntan at the funeral. I also caught a terrible cold, which is still lingering. I wondered whether I had got it the moment I touched my mother's chilly forehead. I reverted to my old-style coughing, such as I had in childhood.

I gazed at the stones with family names. There were already two Josip Novakovics buried here. This was the place where I would end up. My mother should have, by her matrilineal heritage, been buried at the Calvary cemetery in Cleveland, where her mother and grandmother are buried, or in Medjuric, where her father is, by train tracks, and where her brother would be buried.

I walked back with my half-aunt, Djurdjica, who talked about Rutica (Ruthie). Her teacher says she was the smartest pupil he had at the school in thirty years, by far. You never know what she could have become if she had been allowed to continue school after the fourth grade. She could remember everything, she spoke three languages fluently, she could do long multiplications and divisions in her head, and she could think clearly. And then I heard your father was like that in his school and he couldn't go on after the fourth grade either. You are so lucky to get such genes. You and your siblings should all be geniuses.

I suppose we should be, I said, but you never know what environment and spite can do to your head. I didn't say that but in my case, with lung afflictions and oxygen deficiencies and sleep disorders, I am sure I got my brain damaged somewhere along the way, never to live up to my genetic potential.

Djurdjica continued, But the odd thing is that Mother was so shy that when her teacher invited a government official from Zagreb to show how well his pupils were learning, Ruthie wouldn't answer any questions. She turned red and practically mute. The teacher was embarrassed.

Later, after a dinner during which no alcohol was drunk, I talked with my brother and had two glasses of red wine. For a long time my mother had one drink a day and then she lost the taste for it. Djurdjica's mother lived to be ninety-six, and she started every day with a shot of plum brandy. My mother had me taste beer when I was twelve. It was a terribly hot day, and she sweated in the garden, and said, There is only one thing that will quench thirst in this dog heat, and that is beer. Go out and buy us a large bottle of cold beer.

I did that, and she drank half of it, and wanted me to drink the rest, and I found beer bitter and heavy. I don't like it, I said.

During the evening after the funeral, Ivo brought up his theory why our mother didn't believe in praising her children, Ljerka's early death.

Do you know the whole story of her death? Vlado said. I was fourteen then, old enough to follow what was going on. Ljerka got the German measles inoculation. The medicine arrived from the United States. Tito had usually declined donations from the States, and it would have been good if he had declined this one. The inoculation was at the experimental stage, and Americans experimented in the countries where there was no system of lawsuits for health damages, and Yugoslavia was one of them. Eighty children in Yugoslavia developed meningitis and died as a result of this overly strong inoculation. (The inoculation would be modified and approved only thirty years later). Ljerka was one of the victims. Our father went insane over that. When she got sick, he took her to the hospital, and gave a huge sum of money to the doctor, and said, Do all you can to keep her alive for me, will you? The doctor promised he would.

She died the next morning; there was no helping her.

He was struck with grief as was our mother. Only months later did it cross his mind that he had given the doctor a fortune to keep Ljerka alive. The doctor should have had enough conscience to return the money but he didn't.

Father sometimes said, Here I toil for the money I used to have, but those doctor crooks kept it.

So, that's America for you. Later, when an American preacher heard the story he told our father that he should sue the American government for sending faulty medication to Yugoslavia, but Father declined to do that. He always stayed insanely pro-American.

I wondered if I had known this story earlier, whether I would have been so eager to go to the States, which I considered my motherland, since my mother came from there, though her roots were in the borderlands between Slovenia and Croatia, where her parents were born.

When I talked about Mother's shyness, Ljubica said, Oh, she wasn't always shy. I remember how you threw a truck tire in front of an oncoming car. You rolled it and timed it so it smashed the front of the car. The driver ran after you through the streets and couldn't catch you but you ran out of breath and ran home. She protected you and yelled at him what kind of man he was that he wanted to beat a child. You were bad.

That is true, I remember. I had had some delinquent tendencies.

When I mentioned that Mother had a terrific healthy habit of fasting one day a week, every Saturday, Vlado said, She didn't do it for herself. She never did anything for herself. It was for you and Ivo, she prayed and fasted one day a week, so God would protect you and so you'd keep the faith of your fathers.

That is strange.

Yes, you brought her a lot of grief. Well, I must admit, it was not only for the two of you, but for all her children, the five of us, and perhaps for the dead ones too. I do believe it all had a good effect on her health but it was not for her sake she did it. You know, selfishness is basically bad for your health, and altruism is good, and that is why she lived so long, and she would have perhaps lived longer if the last war hadn't shaken her so much.

Ivo and I talked later still, and I said, You know, we were not good sons. After Dad's death, things were difficult for Mom, and we made them more difficult still by being nasty boys.

I agree, he said. We didn't listen to her at all, we were rude, we stayed in the streets past midnight nearly every night while she worried about what we were doing. We were doing nothing bad, really, we didn't drink or have sex, but she had no way of knowing that.

We thought we were exploring the world, ideas, hanging out with friends, and she didn't understand that. She didn't approve of our friends, she wanted us to have the square and studious ones, not the delinquents we tended to.

I know. She wanted me to study, but she could hardly ever see me study. I did read books late at night, and she kept coming to my room and turning off the light, saying, you will ruin your sight. What kind of life will it be if you are blind as a mole?

And what kind of life will it be if I am an idiot who has read nothing?

But what are you reading? Karl May? What good will it do to you, stupid adventure novels.

It was Einstein's favorite reading in his adolescence.

As was math. I don't see you reading math books.

Get lost! I'll read what I want, and if you want to know, my eyes are my strongest feature—my teeth will fall out, I'll grow deaf, by I will still see very well, I just know.

Don't boast lest God should. . .

And we'd quarrel at three in the morning like that. I thought I was in the right, but of course she was. I could have got up earlier and read during the day.

And Ivo was like that too, shouting at her. She was a poor widow with sons who shouted at her and didn't listen to her. She carried flowers to the grave of her husband, and perhaps she wished he was alive because we had feared him. He didn't tolerate insouciance. He beat us to subdue our selfish wills. He beat Ivo more than me and I learned on the example of how to avoid his educational wrath. There was something biblical in his rage—he'd quote from the Bible and beat you. She probably thought we deserved that but couldn't do it, other than when we were smaller to pull us by our ears.

Ivo had an anecdote about Mom in exile, in Switzerland, during the bombing of Daruvar. There was an immigrant child, a couple of years older than Ivo's son Matija. The boy, from Serbia, used to beat Matija, the way we grew up, older boys beating younger boys, animal style, older cats chewing on younger cats, something that looks ugly from the outside but is probably an all right way of growing up. You learn to mistrust people and you also learn authority. Actually, I detest that kind of childhood although it was mine. Anyhow, Ruth came up to this boy, and said, Why do you have ears? Why? asked the boy. To listen. I told you not to torture that poor boy, and you keep doing it. That means, you aren't using your ear. While talking to him, she grabbed one of his ears and twisted it. The boy grew red from pain and cried, and she let him go.

Can you imagine if they had reported that to the Swiss authorities? Ivo said. Child abuse. I don't think the boy complained. He stopped beating Matija.

She always took care of her brood, I said. There's something instinctive and animalistic about that, isn't there?

She pulled us by the ear all the time.

Yes, she had a fetish about it. Her favorite saying was an old Jewish proverb. Why do we have two ears and one mouth? In order to talk half as much as we listen.

She believed we should never talk much, eat much, drink much, say much—basically, she asked for a life of restraint and obedience.

True, Vlado said, but she had courage when it came to survival. She saved her father, who was in prison for anti-communist statements after the war, when Tito had people shot left and right simply because he didn't want to be weaker than Stalin. He was as ruthless. (Ruth-less?) She went to the regional Communist Party headquarters and asked for his release, saying he was unjustly accused. Her argument was that he was a worker damaged by America. He lived in America, worked in a steel factory, joined a union, basically a communist workers' organization, and as an American communist he was not rational, and his statements therefore should be ignored. He came back to his village, alive, after that. She probably saved him. And then she remained the shy woman and mother. I believe that she was actually quite heroic. Nothing physical scared her. Only people and their politics did, and even worse, diseases.

If I am writing an homage to my mother, and I am some kind of writer, I feel guilty at my lack of artlessness and skill. This should be a beautiful story. I stepped out into the woods; it's fall, and after the powerful windstorm last night, the sky is clear, the visibility is fantastic, and the sun is shining through maple and oak balding splendor of yellow and rusty red, while the wind shushes and whispers. He who has ears to hear, let him hear. I should write more in that vein of beautiful images and sounds but what can I say, I listen twice as little as I talk. I have two lips and only one good unplugged ear. The other is still plugged from the combo: airplane and cold.

While standing among the trees and looking up at them swaying and shushing, I wondered, It's one week since my coming back from Croatia, eleven days after her burial, and I am doing this, writing about her and her life and death. Can't I write something else? Is this grief? The hell with it, it probably is. I remember how I feared, as a child, her death. My second nightmare: my father and I are standing next to Mom's casket. He has blue stubble on his chin. I ask, what next? And he says, How would I know? I wake up shrieking, and it turns out I have a high fever. That was my TB year, with lots of fevers.

My first nightmare that I remember, the same year. Ambulance at the gate and Mother carried out on stretchers. I shrieked out, *Bonica.* I skipped an *l,* in *Bolnica,* Hospital, or literally, *the house of pain,* as *Bol* is *pain.* But *Bon* is *good,* so, in a way, in my childhood dyslexia, I said *the house of good,* but it certainly didn't feel like it as I shrieked. My sister, four years older than I, woke up first, and comforted me, and for years, she thought it was cute that I had shouted *Bonica.* (It was my father actually who was carried out the same year for kidney failure.) Now she is a nurse in a cardiac surgery unit in Stuttgart. She was sent to Germany for training at the age of fifteen, to become a nurse. Why not a doctor, I don't know. She was the best student in her class, but so shy that she often covered her eyes with her palm so she wouldn't have to make eye contact. On the other hand, this is a very ostentatious way of not making eye contact—you can always avoid it, you don't have to use your hands, just look at them. I think looking at your hands at the time of challenge and temptation is the best way to stay put and to tell others to stay put.

Nela's main complaint about the funeral was that the morticians didn't use Mom's dentures to prop up her mouth. In the West, you won't let the mouth sink like that, she said.

Vlado looked at her blankly. He took care of Mom for ten years, and she was never there, and she only preached about how it should be done. He didn't say a word. So, is that it, your Mom in a natural state is not properly pretty for you? I exchanged glances with him. I trusted him. When Father died, this was the man who came from Novi Sad, as a doctor, with an olive-colored partisan cap and dark crimson five-limbed star, after nearly bleeding to death himself from a tonsillectomy gone wrong. This was my father's boy, beaten many times by the man. He was the man now. We were lost without him, and it stayed that way.

I remember how when Dad died, I looked up at Mother and didn't say, What's next? It was the end, no father. Even in my nightmare, my father remained as the pillar of safety. But he was no safety. He had no measure in him. She did. I wish she had written, as she had wisdom. I don't have it, I never will, my father didn't have it, although he was a luminous and prophetic kind of musician and enthusiast. He earned her love somehow, so that she remained faithful to him for thirty-nine years after his death, every day looking at their wedding picture. It's amazing. I am not capable of such endurance, and he probably wasn't, but then, did I know him? Did he know himself? Did he have enough time to know himself? A Biblical pacifist, he spent eight years in the army, two before the war, four during it, two after it, totally ruined by the killing fields. I wonder whether he ever killed. I know he was tormented and tortured. His brother boasted that he, as a partisan with a machine gun, had killed lots of people, but was even that true? Dad claimed he shot in the air, that only God could determine who should live and who should die, and he prayed during fire exchange, and he wasn't shot although most of the people around him eventually were shot. Anyway, this is not a tribute to him, but to my mother.

The burial is over, and I don't have to travel to my hometown for a while. I always struggled to get away from home, but there was a home and now there isn't. Naturally, eventually, I will have to buy a plot of land near the graves of my parents. That grave looks a little too tight for me. There are way too many people there, in six square meters. Our bones don't need to cling and clang and scrape together. Another plot of land, with some elbow room, although I am not going to be doing anything with my elbows, is slightly less appalling than this underground bedroom of my parents.

ON RAISING A PRODIGY

MY FATHER TRIED IT. In Daruvar, Croatia, he bought a piano, sat my oldest brother at it, and hired a teacher. Whenever Vlado made a mistake, the teacher caned his fingers. After a few such lessons, Vlado skipped one; the teacher complained and wanted his money. Vlado said he was beaten; the teacher denied it. Father believed the teacher, and beat Vlado for maligning such a gentleman. After that, Vlado made sure not to play the piano again. Father attempted to persuade him a few times with the belt and a stick, which only confirmed Vlado's impression of the piano as the black instrument of torture.

There was no reason to think that I would fare any differently from my father in raising musical progeny when I sat my son at the piano in Cincinnati, Ohio. Actually, because I enjoyed classical music, Joseph had been exposed to it, in a muffled way, in the womb, in Fargo, North Dakota: Mozart, Beethoven, and Stravinsky. He could have heard the bass and the timpani, maybe some deeper cello tones, but I doubt that any of the violin's thin strings stirred his placenta. After his umbilical cord was cut, his chin trembled from the traumatic birth (which lasted for two days), and he cried. I carried him into the room, while his mom was knocked out after the C-section, and the radio emitted a Mozart string quartet with low and perfectly placed vibrations from the cello. He immediately grew quiet and relaxed. Maybe that vibration made him feel at home, like he wasn't completely thrown out into the stingingly bright and cold world. We considered his response a sign from the heavens, and nearly named him Wolfgang. I decided against it since a German name would clash with the Slavic surname. He was named Joseph, not after Haydn, or me, but after his grandfather, and the few generations of forefathers, all Josephs (rather, Josips, but as I would register him as an American, I anglicized the name). Anyway, his music-loving grandfather would be proud of him.

We got a piano at an auction for three hundred bucks, and I dragged it to our apartment. I did it in the middle of a comprehensive heart test, with needles still stuck in my veins for the next drawing of blood. When I bent my elbows, I could see and feel the needle bending. When I got back to the clinic, the cardiologist said the test was perfect, except the heart rate was a bit elevated. I described what I did, and he said, Oh, in that case it's fine. Maybe we should patent piano carrying with needles in your arms as the cardiologic stress test?

Joseph loved rummaging on the keys with his quick fingers, and pretty soon he could poke out all sorts of tunes, when he was five. We failed to find a good piano teacher in Cincinnati—there was a French one down the block but a friend wouldn't give her name out. But, at the downtown elementary school in Cinci, which was ninety percent black, our son got his start on the cello. Mrs. Sherzer—no joke, that was her name—taught him a lesson a week, although the lessons started late in November, when Joseph was almost seven. Before entering the school, Joseph was proud of his speed—he could run fast—but after running on the playground with the inner city boys, he lost that conceit, which freed him up for music.

We rented a tiny cello, one-quarter size, from Mr. Lutovski, on the West Side, on a hill. Cincinnati, like Rome, they said, was built on seven hills. Well, like Rome, it was hot and polluted in the summer. Mrs. Sherzer taught the Suzuki method, and Joseph caught on immediately. The piano was still his stronger instrument, and we thought he could do both.

When we moved to Tennessee for six months, Jeanette, my wife, was so brainwashed by the Suzuki cult that she wouldn't have lessons from the classical cellist who lived next door to us and who played cello sonatas at a reception for the president of the college. The cellist wanted Joseph to work from the notes, and Jeanette thought that working like that was a sacrilege to his ear and memory, and so she drove north of Nashville once a week, for two hours each way, to get lessons from a certified Suzuki cello teacher. By the time Joseph got that far north, he was asleep and tired, and so for half a year the lessons were worthless.

We went together to see Emanuel Ax play Mozart's Piano Concerto no. 21. Since my office was right next to the music hall, I was asked to let Mr. Ax use it for a day, and so we met him right outside my office door. Joseph was extremely shy at that time, and he hid behind me as Mr. Ax, who was all sweaty from a vigorous exercise, talked to him. Mr. Ax approved of the Suzuki method up to the age of nine, but after that, he thought there were better methods. I forgot how he joked with Joseph, but Joseph was terrified.

The piano lessons on a Bösendorfer in the local chapel weren't useful as Steve, his teacher, fixated on getting everything right; they repeated each phrase about fifty times until Joseph began to cry out of sheer boredom.

My teaching him tennis wasn't much more successful. I would insist on the right grip, and the follow through on the swings, so even when he got the balls over the net, I'd have an objection, and he refused to get more lessons. Lessons were clearly no fun. But then he enrolled in a tennis class for kids, and the teacher was patient and positive, and Joseph grew to love tennis, except not with me. Fathers, I learned, can't teach their sons much, unless they practice terror and absolute authority.

At that time we thought of moving to Croatia for two years. I would have to teach in Cincinnati half of each year, and my family could live there full time, and I would commute occasionally when teaching. The reasons for reverse migration were ample—walking culture, good farmer's markets, foreign languages, worsening politics in the States, and finally, music. You could enroll your kid in a music school and get two lessons a week and solfeggio for 120 kunas a month, which, at the time, meant fifteen American dollars. For that you could buy a third of a lesson in the States. And we'd also have the music culture around us, with concerts. First I took him to the Lisinski School for an audition. Joseph played a simplified Bach partita. He wore a black jacket, and had long blond hair, and looked terribly serious as he played. The teacher positioned him, made him sit symmetrically, and exclaimed, Look how beautiful he is! She loved how he played, but more how he looked, and I was impressed by what a good and pretty teacher she was. I reported the success at home, and we checked it with my friend Darko, who taught the piano at the Zagreb Conservatory. I never heard of her, he said. There's a guy there, Crnogorski, who is supposed to be a good teacher, but not the tops.

Who is the tops? Valter Despalj? I asked.

Yes, of course, but I don't believe he teaches young children.

I talked to Despalj on the phone; he was in Zadar doing his Cello Mania conference. Yes, he would listen to our son, but only in November.

What to do till November?

We took him to Blagoje Bersa, a good music school and he passed his audition on the piano and on the cello. Now he took lessons from Svoboda, a Czech girl, on the piano, and Ivancica, on the cello. The two had completely different approaches.

Svoboda—whose name means freedom in Czech—encouraged him to play new repertoire every month, so it seemed more like a course in music reading than in technique. She assigned very little homework. Ivancica held him back to basic tunes, below his level, simply because he played a bit messily, not holding the bow the way she thought he should hold it, and in half a year he grew to resent the cello. Svoboda, however, didn't make the piano his main instrument, as she frequently forgot to show up for the lessons, and never held the lessons beyond the assigned thirty minutes.

Whenever I was in Zagreb, I'd take him to the school, and then sit in the square, Britasnski trg, sipping mineral water, or coffee, or beer, with my friends, or alone, reading the papers, basking in the sun, until he was done with the lesson. Now, that didn't seem a bad way to raise a prodigy, drinking Budvar and retelling the new batch of jokes. Otherwise, my wife would attend to his lessons, and she'd pay extra so Ivancica would come over to our place and teach Joseph at home. The Croatian kids, if they were talented, didn't pay extra, but we were considered American, and Americans have to pay more, that's the worldwide rule. Certainly it held true in Russia.

Then, the first winter, we heard from Ivancica that an amazing teacher from Minsk was coming, Vladimir Perline, to offer a quick seminar. We went to the master lesson. The man, looking a bit like Boris Spasky, had charisma. He'd play my son's little cello perfectly in tune, never missing the pitch. He shouted, grimaced, stuck his tongue out, performed. People said that at home, he held a child out of the window from the tenth floor by his legs, to scare him into playing better. To show the drawbacks of playing stiffly, he grabbed a can of Coke and crushed it in his hand. Everything was a metaphor for him; the arms were wings, and they needed to fly gently. It was a scary experience for all the participants in the program to be publicly humiliated and toyed with by this master teacher. Joseph liked the show. Perline came back next summer to Hvar, and we went there to a program organized by Dobrila Berkovic-Magdalenic. At that time, Dobrila, who was famous for being a good teacher for kids, was Joseph's primary music teacher. She had launched Monika Leskovar, with a bit of finishing schooling by Valter Despalj, and later Geringas. We came to Hvar three summers in a row, and Joseph had fine teachers, such as Boyarski from Moscow and London, and then Schoenfeld from LA, and Laszlo Metzo, a member of the Budapest String Quartet, and Nino Ruzevic, the Zagreb symphony principal cellist. The only problem was that each teacher had a different ideology, so what Joseph learned from one teacher was attacked by the next.

Dobrila was a big boss in the young cellists' world in central Europe. In addition to teaching at one of the best schools during the year, she ran the Hvar program, where many famous cellists came to teach in exchange for accommodation in the island resort, travel, and perhaps an honorarium. Everybody was happy, trying to cool off on the beach and swimming in the azure waters. I am not sure how much concentration the kids could have with all the shrieking on the beaches, heat strokes, constant noise even at night, and gloomy parents, who were stunned by the prices. There were teachers from Poland, and many other countries with bad climates, and lots of students, all either prodigies or aspiring to be or pretending to be. Anyway, it's a worldwide phenomenon now to have classes in music, writing, sports, self-improvement, in most beautiful locations all over the world, to combine hedonism with discipline and learning; and perhaps more importantly, to get top teachers to teach for sub-standard honoraria.

We moved back to the States, but continued to visit Hvar, and also St. Petersburg, Russia, where I taught fiction writing in the Summer Literary Seminars, and which, of course, is swarming with classical musicians. I saw a guy in the street with a cello on his back; he looked serious and gloomy, like a young Dostoyevski. I asked him whether he'd teach our son, and for a good fee he would. The problem was that Dmitriy had never taught a child; he was incredibly insistent on a few technical things, such as a steady bowing motion and pitch. It turned out he had a bad temper; he'd stand up and shout occasionally, and I'd have to translate his insults. But he too had some charisma, and taught Joseph a few things.

Joseph participated in several competitions and won first place awards in his age group at Wagner College in New York; first at the international competition for young cellists in Porec; second at the international competition in Liezen, Austria (twice); first in the greater Pittsburgh competition. When Itzhak Perlman saw him play on a DVD, he admitted Joseph into the Perlman Music Program, where he was the youngest member for two years; usually there were one hundred applications for each spot in the program, and that year there was no space for cellists, but Mr. Perlman made an exception when he saw with what flair Joseph played.

The camp took place for six weeks every summer on Shelter Island; Mr. Perlman's personal chef cooked for the kids. Joseph's chess game and ping-pong improved there, and so did his cello playing.

During the year he attended the Juilliard pre-college program in NYC, which meant that I had to drive him there nearly every weekend. For Joseph it was all right to commute like that—he mostly slept in the car or did his homework, to keep up with his studies as a regular student at State College High.

As a winner of the Gorizzia international competition, he got to play in many venues at the age of nine, including the Mozarteum in Salzburg. Since then he has played at a Perlman Gala event at Carnegie Hall, and he played in the Juilliard Junior Orchestra at Alice Tulley Hall, at the Lincoln Center, and in many other great locations.

The problem for me as a professor, which is to say, a person with a relatively modest income, was to support his prodiginess or should I say prodigality? Maybe prodigy and prodigality are related, and anyhow, they have the same effect: they cost a lot of money. It would be worse if I had to buy him a cello, which eventually I'll have to do; he has won a cello as a free loan for three to four years from the Carlson Foundation in Seattle. However, his bow, for example, is of inferior quality, worth only $800. An excellent bow would be $10,000, and naturally, I am not going to buy it, unless I win some major book contract or a movie deal, which is not likely.

Now I understand the idea of a sponsor. At Hvar, there used to be a lanky old man with missing teeth who tortured his daughters, a violinist and a cellist. He'd shout at them, *bistro, gromko*! He had them play at the public square to raise money, and occasionally he would disappear to Split, and there were rumors of how he employed his daughter there, which I didn't believe, but anyhow, they had occasional meetings with their sponsor in Split, who, for some reason needed to see them frequently. When the old man learned I was from America, he immediately wanted me to be the sponsor of his daughters. I talked to a German cello teacher, who says he hit her up with the same proposal.

Maybe this costly enterprise and systematic torture will eventually pay; maybe he will make a living as a cellist and play in a good symphony and a quartet. He is hitting adolescence, so who knows? Last month he fell and broke his arm. Fortunately, he recovered swiftly, but what if he has a harder fracture? At least he has the math to fall back upon. He does math three years ahead of his age group, and gets As. In Britain, where we sent him for two years to study at the (Henry) Purcell School (with the Russian cellist Vladimir Boyarski as his teacher), he won the Gold Certificate in math. I believe math education is cheap. If we were starting it all over again, I would probably immediately stimulate him just to do math and physics. So far math costs me maybe a hundred bucks a year—for example, he persuaded me to buy a thick book of Euclid's geometry.

Occasionally I marvel at the difference in upbringing my son and I are having. I began to play the violin at the age of thirteen, too late to be a prodigy, and I had a violin with a very crooked neck, which made it hard to keep the right order on the strings, each string having a different geometry. My teacher was the former military band conductor from Belgrade, Malek, who met the Lord and joined our Baptist church. Apparently, the Lord was good at keeping Godspodin or Drug or Brat (Brother) Malek away from the bottle, but not from his anger. If I missed a pitch, Malek would turn red in the face, and he'd start lisping and spittle would spark out of his mouth, his lips would turn purple, and he'd slap me on the wrist with his bow. I wasn't surprised to hear, once I left the country, that this master of controlled rage (such as military marches are), died of a massive heart attack. No wonder my education in the violin went nowhere, and as soon as I broke my hand, just like my son did, I took that as a sufficient excuse to quit playing the violin. I was basically pissing in the sand at the age when my son played Brahms' symphonies and Beethoven's sonatas.

But I didn't have as much talent as my father did. He could play ten instruments and he ran a tambourine orchestra in Andrijasevci near Vinkovci. For relaxation he played the guitar and sang. Maybe talent, which certainly can't be carried over by dominant but rather recessive genes (otherwise we'd all be talented) tends to skip a generation, and to recombine itself later. Maybe we are like plants that way; in good and rare ways resembling our grandfathers, and in bad and common ones, our fathers. I inherited my father's sleep disorders without his music talents. I know, this is too simple, but tempting to believe.

Well, now while my son is at Juilliard in his chamber music program, I am sitting in a coffee shop, and a friend of mine from Russia will join me—so things aren't all that dissimilar from what I'd be doing if I were shepherding my son in the music stalls in Zagreb. Of course, it could all be a terrible waste of time. I am reminded of an anecdote involving one of the Diogeneses in Ancient Greece. Diogenes heard a young man playing on the lute. The otherwise stoical philosopher seemed to be touched by the emotional music and he fought tears. And then, when the young man played a quick and brilliant sequence of sounds, involving very complex fingering, Diogenes burst into tears. Why are you weeping, Master? At first I thought the man spent months acquiring his skill, he answered. Now I realize it's years. I am weeping for his wasted years. The more he plays, the more evidence he supplies about how much time and talent he has wasted.

Sometimes when my son plays an Elgar cello concerto, I am moved, too, and perhaps more by the realization of how much time and money have vanished in the subtle sliding and dipping sounds. The cello is indeed the sad instrument.

Post scriptum, four years later: Three years ago Joseph was furious when he saw that the preceding text was published on a popular Croatian internet site. He said, Don't ever call me a prodigy. I hate that word.

Why?

It's nerdy and it sucks. There are too many prodigies or hardly any, depending on your definition.

I guess you were surrounded by too many prodigies at Juilliard.

No, very few. It makes me feel like a stupid and obedient kid with boastful parents. I am too old for such names. Don't call me names.

For him, prodigy has become a dirty word, a swear-word. I agreed and pulled the article. I am sure he'll be mad when he sees this in print, but the boasting rights have cost me enough, so I will go ahead, and he is out of the danger zone now; he's eighteen. Nobody calls eighteen-year-old musicians prodigies. At any rate, in 2010, after studying with David Soyer (founder of the Guarneri Quartet) at Juilliard—who died during my son's last year, traumatizing him as though he'd lost all of his grandparents at once—Joseph moved to Montreal to study the cello with Matt Haimovitz and math. He says he could already have a master's in mathematics if he hadn't spent so much time with the cello. Since he likes abstract and theoretical math, in which it's hard to get jobs, I tell him jokingly he'd better keep up with his music so he can support his math habit.

FIVE EASY PIECES IN MOSCOW

MOST RUSSIANS DON'T get up early. The shops in St. Petersburg open at ten in the morning, and that holds true even of coffee shops. Perhaps the notion of coffee as wake-up drug in Russia hasn't filtered through the haze of the inimical climates and histories. Sometimes when the coffee shop opens, you can see jaded-looking men and women—literally jaded, a little green and sallow—drinking absinthe. Now that is a way to start the day—no wonder there is a secretion of the liver contributing to the skin color. You may ask for coffee at ten, and the counter clerk most likely will look astonished, and ask, *Espressa*? They tend to turn their *os* into *ah* sounds. Then it may take them half an hour to get the machine working. In the finest St. Petersburg shop, the espresso machine didn't work for two weeks during my stay there. But this is not the story of St. Petersburg but of Moscow, which though more business-oriented and energetic, still has that late-to-bed late-to-rise rhythm, and the train schedule seems to reflect that. The express trains from Moscow to St. Petersburg were scheduled to depart between one am and two am. I got the tickets for the two am train, and since I was indoctrinated by the American airport schedules, which in this era of security demand that the passengers be early and planes late, I wanted to get to the station an hour before departure—

to give ourselves a margin in case we couldn't get a large cab easily. We were four, the whole family, with an additional member, the cello, with its huge case. We went out with our luggage and stood on the curb, next to an all-night kiosk. A few drunks leaned against the kiosk and drank from cans of beer. A small Zhiguli police car was parked nearby, bestowing an air of security on the block. I don't know where the name *Zhiguli* comes from, whether it's a play on the Italian *gigolo,* and whether the car is a copy of a Fiat, but there is definitely a second-hand air even in a new Zhiguli, and the cops looked a little second-hand and disinterested. In fact, they drove off. First a small car stopped, and a mustachioed man stepped out and insisted that all of us, our luggage and passengers, could fit, and was mightily offended when I said we could not fit. He would not charge much, only 150 rubles to the train station. Maybe our luggage would fit sans us. Maybe that was the plan, load up the car and drive off. After a decent amount of shouting, the man left.

Now another mustachioed man stopped with a larger car, a Lada coupe. We all fit, although it was not easy. He had some metal pipes and boxes in the trunk, which he had to spend a few minutes rearranging.

I knew the direct way to the train station, having walked it. Down Koltze, turn left, up a huge boulevard, and that is that, a simple L trip, but apparently, for this man, there was no such thing as a simple line. He drove us up Chapin, and turned right there, into a dark and bumpy street. His gas gauge kept beeping. Nice, he's driving on empty. Maybe there's a gas station here? Maybe he knows how to time everything? That might be a good scenario, to be out of gas, or to pretend to be, and to stop in an alley where his assistants could take our luggage and work us over. No doubt such things have happened.

The cobbles of the street made the tires purr in their loud way.

At the traffic light, the man turned off the car, until the green came back on, and then he cranked on the ignition. Oh no, Jeanette said. But the ignition caught on. Maybe the corner was not dark enough. On the other side of the corner, diagonally, there was another Zhiguli with policemen. At the next corner there was another police car and a couple of policemen standing outside of it.

"All this police!" shouted our driver. "On every street corner. That is too much."

And true, wherever we looked there were police cars. For what, I wondered? I hadn't seen that many police even in NY after 9/11, and this may have been related, a pre-emptive measure.

Our driver was getting more and more incensed at the sight of the police. Why should the police bother him? His being terrified of the police might have made him suspect. On the other hand, I was never particularly fond of them either, in any country, so his displeasure with the arbitrary executors of the law didn't incriminate him in my eyes.

Anyhow, he made it to the train station, and I gave him two hundred rubles, as much as he had asked, and it wasn't that much, six dollars, and he opened up the trunk but didn't help me unload.

At the curb, a young man with a flatbed wooden pushcart offered to take the luggage for one hundred rubles.

That's a lot, said Jeanette. If the cab is only two hundred, this should be less.

That's all right, I said. He probably needs the money.

We loaded a large suitcase, and four smaller ones, and Jeanette carried Joseph's cello.

The porter wasn't officially attired. He didn't have the cap. He was a young somewhat Asiatic looking man, perhaps from southern Siberia, if there is such a thing. Such a huge region should have a south as well as an east. He had a black blazer as though he were a waiter at a fancy hotel and black thin-soled leather shoes which didn't give him much traction, so that as he pushed he slid backward, but he progressed. He didn't go to the side where he could avoid the stairs, but directly forward. He couldn't lift the pushcart over the stairs, and he needed my help. I got the lower, heavier end, but I didn't mind. It entertained me to see him at work. He huffed and puffed as though his job were horrifyingly hard.

He's putting on a show of labor for us, I said.

Why, it must be hard work, Jeanette retorted.

We paused for a second at the huge schedules board until we identified the express to St. Petersburg, departing from the number three platform. The train stretched all the way down the long platform, seemingly almost a kilometer.

We are in the first coach, I said.

That's all the way down, he said.

Yes, I guess so.

He moaned. I can't go that far. You should pay me more money for that.

One hundred is plenty. We'll make it there easily, no stairs.

He pushed fast, so we could barely keep our pace with him. Now we were, in the good American way, almost an hour early. It was just slightly after one. After we left the roofed part of the train station, the lighting was scarce. This was no St. Petersburg, no white nights here. It was quite dark. The platform was inordinately high above the tracks. Naturally, everything in Russia is big—the subway is deeper underground than anywhere else in the world, the tracks are wider, and the platforms are of course, taller, so we naturally veered off from the edges.

How come there are no other passengers around, asked Jeanette.

I don't know. Maybe not many people are traveling.

Here, there were no police either. It seemed bizarre that in the middle of such a crowded city, you'd find this empty space, next to the train connecting that city with the second most crowded city in the country.

We arrived to the end of the train, the last coach, after which there was nothing, not even the engine. There was light in the first window of the coach.

I handed a one hundred ruble note to the porter.

That was a lot of work, said Jeanette. Give him twenty more.

No, that wasn't bad, what, ten minutes?

The porter stood there expectantly, and when I handed him twenty more, he returned it.

What, you don't want that?

It's one hundred a piece. You have five pieces.

No, we said, one hundred for the whole thing.

He said, One hundred a piece.

I said, one hundred, and it was understood, for the whole thing.

Understood by who? It goes per piece. OK, give me four hundred.

No.

What? He was freaking out. He put the one hundred piece back on my suitcase, and said, Give me three hundred. I will not take less.

Isn't that incredible? I asked Jeanette.

Obnoxious. How much is it anyway?

Ten dollars.

That would be decent rate even in the States.

Well, it's not really that much, but it is too much for this country.

I remembered that at the Shermatovo airport in Moscow the mafia cab drivers wanted one hundred and twelve dollars from us to take us to the center of town, and only after much negotiation, did we get the fifty dollar rate, and our friends thought we got a bargain. So, the prices in this country could be high, but it didn't make sense. Teachers got paid only fifty dollars a month. So a teacher would be better off carrying your luggage four times, once a week, at this rate. No, this couldn't be the rate, I decided. After all, a cab in St. Petersburg cost fifty rubles, usually, if you didn't go far.

Four hundred rubles, he said, again. Or ten dollars and a hundred rubles.

I rummaged through my pockets. What the hell, I could give him a hundred more, or even five dollars, the devil take him. But I didn't have that. I had only a five hundred note, and a twenty euro note. I would not give him that much. Now, that was perhaps petty. You travel, you pay, and this was a big city, late at night, we could just be done with it.

I thought, all right, but ten dollars or three hundred rubles should be the absolute limit. Do you have two hundred rubles? If you do, I will give you the five hundred, and that's that. Amazingly good pay.

He rummaged through his pockets. He would clearly do this if he had the money. No, I don't have two hundred. Give me five hundred. It was five pieces, one hundred a piece.

No way. Five easy pieces, I said.

I put the money in my pocket, handed him over a hundred and a two-euro coin.

He returned these.

How much is the euro?

Thirty-five, so it's one hundred seventy rubles, five and a half dollars, all it's worth. That's minimum wage in the States, and this is less than an hour of work.

But he won't take that, Jeanette commented.

He's stupid. At this rate, he'll get less.

I told him as much. This is the best you will get.

You think? He shouted. You fool, *durak*! Give me my money, give me three hundred rubles, or we go to the police.

What nonsense. You have nothing to do with the police.

You think. *Harasho, poshli*! Let's go. He started putting the luggage back on the cart to push it into the station and look for the police.

No, you can't put the luggage back, I said, and I took it off.

Ha, you don't want to see the police! he said.

There's no reason for that. Why drag the luggage all over the station? They will get here eventually.

You think? No, they won't. I know. Give me my money.

You mean, give you my money?

Now this had been going on for fifteen minutes and there still were no passengers.

My kids—Joseph, ten, Eva, six—were tired.

Why can't he go away? asked Eva.

He wants money.

I saw through the window a train conductor, a blond woman with a blue cap. I knocked on the door, but she wouldn't open. This was forty minutes before the departure.

Give me money, shrieked the porter.

I gave you the money. Take it.

One hundred a piece, five *sumki*.

No, I will never give you that.

You must, you *durak*. I will call my partners.

He pretended he would pull out a cell phone. Then he spat and coughed. His spittle was green.

You think he has TB? Jeanette asked. I read about TB in Russia.

I have no idea what he has. He's demented, for sure. He could have picked up the money and brought luggage for someone else, twice already. Do you believe he has partners?

You never know. That could be unpleasant, she said.

I imagined the scenario, his partner thugs, coming out of the dark and attacking us. How would they know where he was without a phone? They could observe him. Maybe he has to pay money to them.

He put two fingers from both hands into his mouth and blew air and whistled.

His technique was good—the whistle was loud and even seemed to echo from another train. He waited silently, admiring the echo, or waiting for someone to react to the call.

I thought, what the hell, let me see if they show up.

Nobody showed up. He looked down the platform. Here they come, he said.

I looked. There was a group of four, and they walked slowly, carrying heavy luggage. They were Asian, two men, a woman, and a child.

I laughed. These are your partners?

Yes, he said.

They look like travelers.

They are travelers, he said. They could probably change your money.

Go ahead, ask them, not a bad idea.

Give me the five hundred bill, and I'll ask them.

Just ask them, and if they have the change, I'll change with them.

He went to them and talked. They didn't utter a word. They turned their back on him and walked back.

He came back, and said, Give me my money.

What, your partners won't give you any change? I laughed.

They went to call the police to get you, he said.

You think I believe that?

Now he spat and coughed and grew incensed, and came close to me, leaning into my face. He was shorter than me, and I thought, I could grab him by the throat, or punch him, but what would that lead to? If we had a fight, and I beat him, the police would show up and I'd be in trouble. If he proved very quick and we had a big fight, we could both injure each other. Maybe he has a knife? Why should he be so insistent and cocky?

Give me money, or you will die! he shouted.

Now, that is too much. I am not going to give you anything, you idiot, I shouted at him.

Death, death! he shouted.

You think this works? Your threats are nonsense, you are an idiot, here's your one hundred, and go to hell!

Now my kids cried. Daddy, what is going on?

He's a madman, I said.

Hey, look, you aren't ashamed? These are little kids, and you want them to be terrified?

Give me the money, right now, he spat again. He felt inside his jacket as though to ascertain that his gun was still there.

Move away from him, you'll get TB or he'll knife you.

No such thing. I might hit him if he keeps it up.

I knocked on the door. The train conductor put down the blind, obviously wishing nothing to do with this dirty encounter of dirty Americans and porters.

Just go away, I said to him, and offered him one hundred and twenty rubles and two euros—close to two hundred rubles. He put the twenty ruble note back on the red piece of luggage and the two euro coin right over the note. He slid the one hundred note into his pocket and shouted, Two hundred more!

Go away. You got all you'll get. You could have got more but you are crazy.

Give it to me or I'll kill!

You know what, you are an idiot, I shouted at him. Let's go to the police. Right now! *Poshli.*

I grabbed the big red piece of luggage. Come along! I said. We don't even need your damned cart. We can carry it all ourselves. Jeanette grabbed the other luggage.

Now, this had a strange effect upon him. He grabbed his pushcart, panted frantically, and leaped off with it from the platform, and ran over the large gravel pieces to the next side, scrambled to get up, and ran off into the dark.

What? He's gone? I asked.

It looks like it, Jeanette said.

Strange, he bluffed all the way along. When we really meant police, he didn't want to see them.

Of course not. He probably doesn't have the license to work as a porter.

What, does he just come out occasionally at night to torment foreigners?

Probably.

And now as soon as he was gone, passengers strolled down the platform and after them two policemen. The front door opened, and the female attendant invited us in. Why hadn't she done that before? A policeman walked out of the next coach. Was he there all the way through? What was he doing? Sleeping? Flirting?

We got into our sleeping car and stretched out the beds. My throat was dry and sore. I had shouted just as much as the porter; the confrontation had got me more nervous than I thought. I couldn't fall asleep, but kept going over the encounter and imagining how it would have been if I had punched him in the face, let's say if I bloodied my knuckles on his teeth. Would that have felt good? Or would I now be interrogated by the police, imagining at the same time that my blood should be tested for hepatitis? The gall that man had! Or should I have let go of the five hundred, sixteen dollars, and not experienced the annoyance? That would have been better but would have felt like robbery, a minor one but still, a robbery. Well, tourist robbery, with a surcharge for being an American late at night.

We need water, Jeanette said.

You are right about that, I said.

I walked down the platform to the first kiosk in the station, and bought two bottles of water. I handed the five hundred ruble note and wondered whether I would get the exact change back. I got 460 rubles back, quite fine. If I had bought the water first, I would have had the change, and I would have given three hundred to the porter, and the nearly half hour long shouting match wouldn't have taken place. Now, that was a strange way to practice one's Russian. I was surprised in retrospect that at no point had I been confused by his Russian or he by mine. For such intensely packed and alert conversation, one would pay thirty dollars an hour, so for half an hour, the five hundred rubles would have been quite fair, in the States, that is.

I thought the man was completely in the wrong. However, when we got back to Moscow, we had even more luggage, and now it was the middle of the day (we wanted to spend at least one evening in Moscow), and as a porter with a large pushcart—uniform and officer's cap and all—came toward us, I wanted his help although I thought I was done with porters. I read the sign on his cart, fifty rubles per piece of luggage. Ah, so they do count it per piece? In other words, when the thug porter said one hundred, he did mean right away, one hundred per piece, and since I said yes, he could expect to get that, no matter how unfair the price was, and at one in the morning, perhaps the normal price was the double of the day price? Or at least, the porter could aim for that? This current porter took five pieces of luggage of ours and walked in a measured way to the exit and down the walkway and he needed nobody's help. He ran into another porter who had twenty pieces of luggage—in other words, one thousand rubles right there on the cart. That porter asked, What, only five pieces?

A job is a job.

So, totally ungrudgingly, I gave him 250 rubles, and then tipped him fifty. The man made three hundred in five minutes, which was fine. He got us to a cabby, and here a new round of negotiation started. The cabby wanted five hundred. Five hundred? I said. Normally it's two hundred.

But there are four of you, and you have so much luggage, and my car is a Volvo, he said.

You got a point, but . . .

OK, will you cut it out? Jeanette said. Let's just take it.

Three hundred, I said.

Four, and that's the best I can do for you, said the cabbie.

Fine, no problem. We sat in the car and five minutes later we were at our address, and the cabbie helped us unload and asked why my Russian was so good.

It's not that good, I said. I've had good lessons, though. low and perfectly

SUMKA 43 — A CAPTIVE CELLO

THE CELLO CAME to our home (Warriors Mark, Pennsylvania) in a carton box, wrapped up in a lot of plastic filled with air. Not the best way to travel if you are a hundred and twenty years old, and indeed, the cello had two long cracks that hadn't shown in the sales pictures. But since we didn't take a photo right away while unpacking the cello, we couldn't get the damage insurance. We considered returning the cello to the sellers in London, but even in its wounded state, it was way too beautiful and resonant not to keep. It had a deep reddish golden color, the color of Montezuma gold, as though it had traces of blood in it. The backboard was flamed; the widely-separated creases displayed the years of the wood; the tree constituting the cello had been a good drinker and fast and vigorous grower, and consonant with that, it sounded boisterous and chesty, just like a confident entertainer holding court.

My son Joseph, who was almost ten, tested the sound. He tuned the cello pensively, leaning his ear against the instrument's neck. He stroked the strings, two at a time. The strings, once aligned perfectly, rang. The intensity of the sound, of all the strings in accord, could tell you that the cello was tuned. This cello was much better than the previous one, which he was renting from his teacher in Croatia, who called it My Strad. Hers was a three-hundred-year-old cello, with a dozen cracks running longitudinally. With a change of temperature, the cracks had widened, and it was impossible to keep the boards together. Bucar, a cello maker in Zagreb, spent weeks attempting to do that—he took the cello apart, glued it, even inserted a bit of old wood to cover a big crack, and put the boards into a press. We had paid for the repairs, and on that account, could use the cello for a year. Despite the cracks, the cello sounded noble, and Joseph won two second place awards in international competitions with it, in Gorizia, Italy, and Liezen, Austria. In Italy, he got a special prize as the most talented of the youngest competitors. After that, we took his cello-playing even more seriously. He used to be a shy boy, who covered his face with his hands if you looked straight at him, but the cello helped him overcome stage fright, and now he became a poised performer, an exhibitionist.

Joseph's teacher in PA, Kim Cook, was the only one not to be seduced by the ancient looks and sounds; she said the "Strad" cello was no good, inaccurate, untunable—and part of the intonation inaccuracies Joseph had she attributed to the irregularities of the cello. And true enough, on this new cello, Joseph's intonation seemed to be cured instantly. He sounded sharper (not in the key pun way). Authenticity and authority came out of that wood, as though a cathedral organ's four pipes were hidden somewhere in the cello belly, ventriloquating.

You wouldn't expect that kind of old-worldly authority to have come out of the Ethernet. The violin-cello had arrived via eBay. How can you trust eBay? I had asked Jeanette.

Why not? Just look at the picture! The sellers guarantee that it's been appraised at Sotheby's of London at one thousand pounds minimum, and they set a reserve price of one thousand dollars.

She had offered less, and the last thirty seconds of the auction she offered one thousand.

How come nobody else in the whole world offered more if it's that good? I asked. I wouldn't buy it that way.

How would you buy it, considering we are stuck in the middle of the boonies, and in the stock market bubble? Where else will you get a centurion cello?

From Witowski in Cincinnati.

He'd charge you three thousand for something like this.

Anyhow, right after the arrival of the newcomer cello, we went to Cincinnati, and visited Witowski in his shop stuffed with hanging pale unvarnished violins and cellos-in-progress. He used to rent us cellos and sell us bows when Joseph was in a Suzuki program in Cincinnati.

Witowski was outraged that we could buy a cello over the internet. He found the idea sacrilegious. These days, however, you can buy even the relics of various saints on eBay, bottled air from the tomb of Jesus, a flame from the burning bush of Moses, so why not a vintage cello?

After grunting, sighing, knuckling the backboard, and scratching his shiny dome, Witowski admitted that the instrument was quite fine for a three-quarter size training cello, and he was amazed that we had got it for only a thousand dollars. He however didn't have time to repair it. To me there was nothing "only" about one thousand dollars since this was the beginning of expenditure.

We got the best strings we could get, at nearly a hundred dollars a set, bows, and expensive lessons. Moreover, every summer we took Joseph to St. Petersburg in Russia, where I teach at the Summer Literary Seminars, and he takes lessons with a member of the Nevsky String Quartet, Dmitry. We got Dmitry's lessons in a peculiar way. First we had asked a friend of ours, a well-known Russian poet, Arkady Dragomoschenko, to find us a cello teacher, and he found a violinist instead. What's the difference? he said. They all know the strings.

In the streets, right after a bunch of Uzbeki children stole our kids' hamburgers and fries, a thin young man with a bony face was carrying a cello case on his back along the Moika River, not far from where Rasputin was clobbered to death. I asked whether he would teach my son. He agreed to teach Joseph for fifteen dollars an hour. Soon we raised his fee to twenty since like many Russian teachers he had no concept of time and his lessons could last for two hours. He was strict with Joseph's intonation and rhythm, and assigned a lot of *gami*, scales. At almost every turn, he'd exclaim, *Uzhasna!* Horrible. Joseph was not perturbed. I told him if Dmitry ever said, *Ochen harasho*, very good, I would give Joseph a hundred bucks. It took seven lessons before Dmitry said, *Da, ochen harasho.* Joseph laughed and Dmitry didn't know why, and for the rest of the lesson Joseph played terribly.

Joseph improved despite all the negativism of the Russian's teaching. Things are never good enough for Russians. Even Eva, our daughter, age five, had to deal with that. We found a ballerina who would teach her some basic steps and postures, and the ballerina told us how she was trained with a stick. Whenever she made a mistake she was caned, until her posture was beaten into shape. So before the first lesson, Eva ran into the small park in the large courtyard where our rented apartment was and came out with a stick. If that's what it took, she was willing to do it. Of course, the lessons didn't proceed with the stick, at least not a physical one.

Convinced we had the best teachers around, we went to admire Dmitry's playing at the Shermatov Palace, and that made a big impression on Joseph, to see his teacher play Grieg and Tchaikovski so deeply in old splendor.

I told Dmitry that the Grieg quartet was far more exciting than the Tchaikovski second string quartet, and he replied that he as a Russian could not say that—since Tchaikovski was a Russian deity.

To further Joseph's music education, I took him to many concerts at the Shostakovich Hall. (Joseph has the misfortune of coming from a nonmusical family. On the other hand, if his parents were musicians, I am sure he would refuse to play—music is a world of his. Even early on, when he played the piano, at the age of six, I flattered him, and said, This is a difficult piece. He replied, How would you know? True, I said, I wouldn't.) We saw Penderecki conduct his Triple Cello concerto—an amazing treat to see one of the greatest living composers conduct his own work. The concerto was full of surprising moves, Baroque-like fugues, Stravinsky-style timpani, Shostakovich jazz. . . The three cellists, all winners of the Tchaikovski competitions, flung their arms and bows up after each long phrase. Penderecki stood on the podium, big and august, so big in fact that he seemed to me a candidate for a heart attack, but these days, with Lipitor and good medical care, he could last, I imagine. Moreover, conducting seems to be the healthiest sport—conductors on average outlive athletes of any kind.

Last year when Dmitry went on tour with his quartet to Germany, we walked to the Anichkov Palace—there was supposed to be a school for gifted children there—on the Fontanka River. We were warned by the babushka at the entrance that the school was closed for the summer, but after I talked with her she said that there was a cellist at work. On the way, we strayed into a tambourine director's office, and he lit up when he saw Eva making her ballet steps and wanted to draft her, offering her a cute balalaika. (Though we said no, there was no time for that, Eva never forgot that moment, so we had to get her a balalaika later on). Disappointed, the director sent us to the cello teacher. She seemed to be around fifty, dressed in an old-style worker's blue uniform. She was teaching two lanky girls. She said to Joseph, Sit down and show us what you can do. My son refused.

If you want to be a cellist, you can't be shy. You get a chance to show your goods, you take it.

I don't want to play on another cello, Joseph replied.

We lived only five minutes away, on the Fontanka, and so we managed to come back with his cello in fifteen minutes. Joseph played the Prelude to Bach's *First Suite* and a Samartini *Etude*.

Good, she said. You have a basis, you have the feeling, but you don't play the scales. I can tell by the upper ranges, your pitch is uncertain. *Nada igrati gami!* You must play the scales. She proceeded to play the D major scale in many variations, with different bowing. She wouldn't receive any money for the lesson. She said, I am scared. I can't do it on the job.

Why don't you come to our place?

I am scared. It is not safe. My husband wouldn't approve.

That's not a compliment to me, I said.

It's just a principle. I could tell you stories; I have had bad experiences.

She suggested, however, that we could bring her a present, and we did, a bottle of good cognac, after which she had her husband's approval to come to our place. I don't know why a taste for alcohol was reassuring to the suspicious husband.

Joseph claimed she gave him superb lessons—she sang for him the pitch of each note he needed to get right. Instead of interrupting his playing, she would lean over and slide his fingers into the right place. She told us how her lessons with Rostropovich went. He was more interested in telling anecdotes and holding court than in teaching technique. It was other teachers in Moscow who really taught. She liked Joseph's playing, but claimed he needed to get stronger, to do push ups, chin ups, to swim, and play tennis to strengthen his arms. Cello playing is not only an art, it is also a sport, she said. You have to be strong. And you must eat well. Eat!

That sounded peculiar to me, a cello teacher uttering the words of a gym teacher. No point in being a frail and effete musician. I remembered seeing a Ukranian woman pianist in Baltimore, Kravchuk, play Tchaikovski, *First Piano Concerto*. She had amazing shoulder muscles, like a weight lifter, and those didn't seem to do any harm when she played the strong chords, plowing through the keyboard.

Joseph, you have a beautiful cello, Tatiana said at one moment. It sounds great. In our country it's hard to get such a good cello for children.

Dmitry, when he came back, looked at Joseph's cello, and said, This is wonderful. I didn't have such a good cello when I was a kid. Yes, you have fine instruments. Now make sure that you play fine.

And Joseph was proud. When he played, the cello seemed to be an extension of his left arm. And he played at many places—at our party, for my class, on the boat on the canals, in front of the Yussupov Palace. It was a beautiful sound and sight—the boards of the boat reverberated with the cello. He played in the lobby of the Herzen Inn. The big hall filled with the gorgeous sounds, and Joseph, letting his blond hair loose, had the cocky poise of a rock star.

Our cello has traveled. We don't know its peregrinations in the one hundred and twenty years before it came to us (Can you imagine all the wars, upheavals, it has witnessed through the fingers of a dozen generations of pre-adolescent boys and girls?) but with us alone, it has done plenty. Now we took it by train from St. Petersburg to Moscow. The trouble with traveling with a cello in a large case is that you need extra space, so even the cabs we took had to be large.

We spent the night at our friends' place—John and Resa, American ex-pats. There are hundreds of thousands of Americans expatriating and exfoliating all over the world, and thousands in Russia, strangely enough, or perhaps it is because of strangeness that they are there.

Trained by American security, I strove to arrive at the airport two hours before the departure of the flight. Considering the impression I got of Shermatovo II, the main Moscow airport, that seemed to be cutting it close, as the customs and security lines seemed to be even longer than the ones at JFK. Moreover, just a few days before, there had been a double-suicide bombing by two Chechen women, which killed some eighteen people and injured fifty, at another Moscow airport. I saw the footage displaying severed arms and heads on the asphalt. The paramedics dealt with all that by simply drawing a big plastic sheet over the whole scene so nobody would have to look at the dead. They seemed to have no interest in checking whether any of the mangled bodies were alive. Moscow is not a good place to be in a critical condition, but perhaps it's a fine place to be dead.

The day before our departure, there was another terrorist attack, which only injured a few people, and there was a successful mafia hit in St. Petersburg, with two bosses dead. The bosses of defeated sections get dumped in the Lutheran cemetery, the most neglected cemetery on Vassilievsky's Ostrov. The cemeteries in St. Petersburg tend to be more beautiful than the living quarters, and the Lutheran cemetery, with the neglect—unkempt trees and bushes, tombstones cracking from extremes of temperatures so you could see into many of the graves, deep into the dark—is the most spookily beautiful. Here resentment against the Germans who had held the siege during World War II that resulted in a million dead is expressed in total neglect. Anyhow, we didn't worry about Chechen terrorism on the way and we couldn't care less where the bosses would be dumped. We were at the airport quite early, more than two hours before our departure.

A customs officer, an elderly woman dressed in green, stopped us, and spoke in Russian. What is that?

A training cello.

Do you have the certified papers for it?

No, we didn't know we needed them for a child's training cello.

You must have the papers. If you don't, go to the Ministry of Culture to have it inspected.

We don't have the time. Our flight is coming up.

That's your problem. Go to the Ministry of Culture.

Is there anybody at the airport who deals with that?

Lost and Found Luggage. They specialize in things like this.

What, is there someone who can certify the cello as not too valuable there?

We are done. I have nothing else to tell you.

People talk about bribes in Russia, and of course, there are bribes all over the place, but she didn't seem to be looking for a bribe. Otherwise, she would have been more approachable. I looked at her from a distance. What was her game? Was she doing her job scrupulously? If we weren't Americans, would she be so unyielding? She looked in her plain dress like someone in the old system, a good Soviet. And I said so to Jeanette, Nothing has changed for many people here. These guys are still Soviets.

This is horrible. They won't let us leave with our own cello?

Maybe we'll find something at the Lost and Found Luggage, though it doesn't sound good.

So we went to the lost and found. In fact, there was a sign in English, LOST AND ABANDONED LUGGAGE. We talked to the three ladies who ran the place, and they all nodded their heads sadly. It probably was not the first cello that ended up there. They suggested that we go to *Nachalnik smjeni*, the shift manager, and talk to him.

What do you think? I asked. Are they just play-acting and they are all involved in this rip-off game?

They seem quite honest to me, said Jeanette.

We found the airport manager. The man listened to our story sympathetically.

OK, I will go talk to customs officers.

He went but there was no conversation between them taking place. Whenever he came close to her, she turned her back to him, her arms akimbo.

He came back. (Veni, vidi, vici. I came, I saw, I *conquered*.) She refuses to talk to me. She says the case is closed.

But you are the airport manager! You are the boss.

I have no jurisdiction over them. They are their own system.

Who else can we talk to?

Malev. The airline people could perhaps do something about it. I will give them a call.

And he did, he dialed them up on his black phone.

So we waited for the airline people. Didn't show up. Time was running out. Would it make sense to go to the something-to-declare line? I asked the *nachalnik*.

I doubt it. You can try, but I doubt it.

I went to the line nevertheless, and the customs officer said, Don't talk to me. If you keep talking I will have you arrested. You don't have a certificate, and you can't get it here.

In the background, we saw the customs supervisor—she was laughing and talking with two young officers. Were they laughing about us? Did it give them joy to make a boy of ten cry for his cello?

The Malev flight to Budapest was being announced. It was unnerving. Do you want to stay in this country to fight for the cello? It could cost a lot of money—changing all the flights. Should I stay behind? I was not in the mood to stay behind. My old mistrust of borders and police kicked in. If I stayed behind, what would guarantee that I could win the right to take out the cello? I was suddenly tired of Russia, though just an hour earlier we all seemed to love Russia, happy with our visit, the music, and the rest.

The customs supervisor was gone. So we went again through the departures line, and the officers, two men, said, Stop, you can't go through. You don't have the papers. We know about you.

But it is our cello, we came into the country with it.

That may be the case, but you can't prove it without the certificate.

But it's a cheap training cello, and only the goods above one thousand dollars must be declared, said Jeanette.

You must read the rules and regulations of a country before you visit it.

At that rate, we'd visit Russia in three years, I said. Who could possibly know all your rules!

You will learn them. We will teach you.

We read the declaration form before we came in, said Jeanette.

It is not that simple, you need to have a certificate for any antique you bring into the country. Westerners have plundered our treasures already.

But it is a simple cello, no point in treating it as an antique.

We are not experts. Go to the Ministry of Culture.

Just look at it, said Jeannette. How do you say cheap?

Deshevo, I said.

In the meanwhile, I thought I saw a Malev employee, so I went away a few paces. I heard the ringing of Joseph tuning the cello. Hundreds of people started to gather. The guards looked furious. Joseph struck the first notes of Tchaikovski's *Nocturne* and wept. If he needed to get the feeling right, for the piece, the sorrowful longing, he got it now.

Enough. Stop right now, shouted the guard. Or you will all be arrested. Stop! Jail, prison, you hear me?

Joseph wanted to say goodbye to his cello. This reminded me of a boy in my hometown who leapt into the grave to kiss the wood of his mother's coffin before the soil could thud over it. There was that sensation of desolation, of nevermore, with the police closing in on our holy wood. The cello sounded soulful and majestic—the airport acoustics were splendid—and that wasn't helping our point that it was just a cheap piece of junk, a learning cello for a kid.

Jeanette packed the cello back into its blue case, and she also took out two bows.

You can't take the bows either, the guards said. They must stay with the cello.

Why? Where is that rule written?

Maybe they need the whole set for their nephews, I said. Anyway, don't argue with them.

I guess we can't bribe them or anything, Jeanette said.

The supervisor probably wants to make sure they don't let us through, and if they did, she would sack them.

We took the cello one floor below, to the Lost and Abandoned Luggage department. Jeanette took out the two bows, each worth about two hundred bucks, and put them in our big suitcase. Would the customs officers notice the bows and freak out? We looked at the case. Maybe we should take the case? We registered the piece of luggage, the cello, as Bag # 43 (*Sumka* 43).

Luckily, I still had a few minutes left on my cell-phone calling card. I called our friends, John and Resa, and told them what had happened. Could they come to the airport and retrieve our Sumka # 43?

Yes, but not right away. We have a lot to do today.

I will understand if you don't do it. We'll send you the cab money. (Cabs in Moscow, to the airport at least, are more expensive than in NYC.)

So, I explained to the old ladies that a friend of ours would come by to pick up the cello.

Good idea, said one of them.

How much do I need to pay?

Forty-eight rubles for one day (a dollar-sixty).

Can I pay for more than one day?

Not necessary.

(What, they weren't angling for bribes either? I was disappointed.) What if my friends take two days to get here?

Not necessary. *Ne nada.* (If one looked for a similarity with Spanish, it would sound like doubly nothing.) Give us your passport number and we'll register the *sumka.* (Actually, *nada,* besides *necessary,* also means *hope.*)

I wrote down John's last name on the little tag on the cello case. Later I regretted I hadn't also written his name by mine in the registration form.

Would the cello make it? Wasn't this just a setup for stealing cellos? Won't now one of those customs guys come downstairs to confiscate the cello, to take it home? Will they also take note of my passport number, put me on some sort of list, not let me into the country the next time? At this rate, I wouldn't miss Russia. We had thought of perhaps buying an apartment in St. Petersburg, but now it was clear that might not be such a good idea. If we didn't have a proper stamp on a piece of paper, we might lose the apartment altogether.

Joseph cried as we walked through. The customs officers now didn't look at us at all. People filed by. We were their torture quota for the morning. Joseph kept weeping.

Don't cry, I said. Worse things could have happened.

Yeah, like what?

Like a bomb going off right now and killing us, like losing an arm, like losing a lung. I can think of a million worse things that can happen. .

I can't.

Besides, John will pick up the cello, so next time you come to Russia, you will have your Russian cello. (I didn't believe what I was saying but it was good to have some *nada.*)

But now I have nothing.

We'll get you a cello in Zagreb.

Worse things could happen indeed. Joseph had an old picture in his passport with short hair, and now he wore long hair. His baby face had elongated. Instead of a little pug-nose, now he had a straight thin one. The policewoman looked at him and at his passport many times, and said, You are Joseph?

Yes, of course.

You don't look like Joseph.

His hair grew long, that's all, I said.

She kept looking at him sternly, making her thin lips thinner.

You just don't look like Joseph. How do I know you are Joseph?

Just look at the features, I said.

Don't tell me what to do. I know my job.

She stared at him.

Are you you?

What, now they wouldn't let us take our son out of the country either? What insanity was that? How do you prove that you are the same person the papers claim you are?

My God, said Jeanette. Is this for real?

We had run into skeptical people. Maybe it had to do with our being Americans—if I don't look American, the rest of my family does, and it certainly sounds American. I could understand what the customs had to deal with. You could come into the country with a kid's passport, and then find a similar kid, and take him along—buy him, steal him, whatever. Sure, that could happen.

See Joseph, worse things could happen.

Just a *shutka*! the officer said. We have to joke now and then, life is too boring.

The customs officer let us through, and soon we were sitting in the very last seats of not the Malev, but of Aeroflot. If the aircraft at least were Hungarian, we'd feel freed. As long as we were in the Russian plane, we were not out of Russia, and worse things could happen.

From Zagreb, later that day, I emailed John and Resa, and said that maybe it would be a good idea to go to the airport as soon as possible. I knew that was an obnoxious request since they were tired. They replied that they could go in the middle of the next week.

Next week! By then the cello would be stolen for sure, I thought, and emailed them to at least make a call to the Sahranyenya department. The Russian storage word sounded like funeral, *Sahrana*, in Croatian, and no doubt, *Sahrana* was a euphemism, meaning storage, just as Russian for cemetery, *Skladbische*, sounds like *Skladishte* in Croatian, *storage*. The whole thing sounded like a funeral to me, and at the time I wished that Joseph had got to play the *Nocturne* by Tchaikovski. He had learned the words of sorrow there too well. Dmitry insisted that certain passages should be played in a weepy way, as though you were devastated with hopeless love. And Joseph was.

We got another three-quarterssize cello in Zagreb—freshly handmade, from Bucar, who first took us on a tour of the hills around his hometown, showed us on a map where the wood came from in Bosnia, claimed it was the same wood that the Italians plundered for their Amati and Stradivarius, showed us his attic where he'd aged the wood for twenty years, got drunk in the process, soulfully canonizing the wood. As soon as Joseph grabbed the new cello, tainted in fresh red varnish, looking like a bloody plump toddler, he played the *Nocturne,* and it sounded like a salute to his old friend.

At this point, we all gave up on the old cello. Sure—Russian border police were evil people, they stole, they loved to torment.

Strangely enough, three days later, John and Resa emailed that Sumka 43 was in their hands. The three kind babushkas had guarded it, and certainly nobody could come close to it. They had examined and re-examined John's passport, comparing the name on it with the name I wrote on the cello, before they released the cello. That was a moment of joy. Joseph—you have your cello back! Well, at least in Russia. So when we go, you don't have to carry a cello to Russia.

We need to get a passport for the cello. We took pictures of the birthing moment, or the baptism, the varnishing, of Joseph's new cello. We'll sign all kinds of papers, maybe we'll even read the zodiac for the cello. July 13, Cancer. It makes sense. We will have to certify our new family member. Cello is not just a thing, it is a member of the family. Even the ruthless police know that, why didn't we? We will get him—does a cello have gender?—a shiny photo.

And what name should we give to the captive cello? It's not an Amati, we don't know the maker; it's an orphan in that sense, and in many others. Should the name be German (since the cello was made in Germany) or English, Russian, Croatian? I will ask Joseph what name he wants to give it. At the moment, he's having a cello lesson with Laszlo Metzo, from the Bartok String Quartet, on the island of Hvar in the Adriatic. There is the smell of smoke all around us, because the island is burning; thick smoke is rising from the hill behind us. The smoke is stinging my eyes.

I'm imagining what the unnamed émigré cello is doing. John and Resa have loosened her strings, put her up high on their shelf, and there she lies, without music, silent, and who knows when she will get to sing her nocturnal feelings again.

BLUE NOTE

WHILE LIVING IN NEW YORK for a year in 2001/02, I wanted to hear top-notch jazz live. Before coming to the States from Croatia (then part of Yugoslavia), I considered jazz to be the ultimate music form, with freedom of invention at every turn, unlike in strict, preordained classical music. While I never managed to buy American jazz, I had several albums of Russian jazz, fabulous quartets and quintets, which I had got in exchange for a complete set of stamps from the forties imaging Tito in profile (it was probably worth more than I knew as it was hard to collect). Eastern Europeans excelled at their breed of jazz and other ghetto sports (basketball, for example); well, Eastern Europe was a huge ghetto, so the music, with its aura of liberation, was quite appealing—it was a form of not only musical but also geographic transcendence. You could travel through sound to Harlem, New Orleans, Chicago; talent and good taste was the visa for the trans-Atlantic flight, and even for the trans-Siberian train. So when I came to the States in 1976, one of the first things I accomplished was to listen to Oscar Peterson. Gradually, as years went by, my fascination with jazz (and rock) and freedom diminished, but the fascination could be easily revived, as could most youthful passions, with the added beauty of nostalgia.

I was a little intimidated by prices: twenty-five dollars a set at Blue Note, a jazz bar, with ten dollars per drink. In other words, a relaxingly tipsy evening would cost about a hundred dollars. Still, we live only once, and that certainly was a loud feeling in New York after 9/11, so with my friend Jeffery Allen, a black writer, I went to listen to the James Carter Trio with the bass-saxophonist David Murray as a special guest. Blue Note, on 4th Street in the Village, is located a few yards away from the subway entrance to the A train. I lived at the last A train stop north, beyond Harlem, and my friend lived near the last stop south, in Far Rockaway, where an American Airlines plane had fallen. Jeff had recently published a big novel, *Rails under My Back,* which won a few prizes; he writes in black slang in very fresh and original sentences. Despite his talent and recent successes, Jeff has remained humble, nearly the only easygoing and normal person at the Center for Scholars and Writers, and the two of us became friends—often having lunches and occasionally going to parties, such as an Indian drummers' party. He grew up in the slums of South Chicago; his alcoholic father left the family when Jeff was four years old, and though he was a big boy, he could not play sports because of his asthma. . . and so he had to do something different; he wrote and played music. Writing won out, but he still yearned for good music. As for me, I wanted to play rock as a kid, but I realized that the moments I enjoyed most in rock, such as long improvisations by Hendrix in "Machine Gun," were jazzy. By the time I wanted to play jazz, I broke my left arm, so that was the end of playing, but certainly not of listening and admiring the art of musical invention.

There was a small line, ten people or so, waiting on the sidewalk to enter the dark jazz club before the second set. It was not surprising that there were so few people waiting. Jazz has become a sort of subculture. It's not a mass culture—the record sales and attendance can't compare with those of

Britney Spears and other pop culture mega and multimedia stars, although of course the quality in jazz is higher. And that is not only a matter of taste but of complexity—Spears sings ditties, and jazz players make amazing musical combinations and variations.

Jeff and I asked to sit right next to the stage, and the waitress who assigned the seats accommodated us. We sat on the same side of the table in order to face the musicians; otherwise one of us would have had to crane his neck to see what was going on. There were some hundred and fifty visitors, and at the table next to us sat a group of young Japanese enthusiasts. James Carter, dressed tidily in black shiny shoes, a three-piece suit, and a tie, came on stage, smiling and shining, more like a young preacher in a black Baptist church than a musician. There was no hint of sin about him. However, David Murray came on stage with his shirt hanging out, and his eyelids half drawn over his eyes, in the manner of Sam Perkins from the LA Lakers, Sleepy Sam, who had one of the best three-point shots.

This guy looks completely stoned, I said to Jeff.

Don't worry, they all are, he replied. David looks like he's taken some heavy shit.

The drummer, in dreadlocks, bony, with big shining eyes and a blissful grin, certainly looked stoned.

There was an announcement that during the set there should be no conversation; this was a concert. We had already got our drinks, I had Brooklyn Wheat (you can finally get small brewery beer in the States that matches the best in Europe, and of course, it has to come out in small editions, just as jazz concerts come out with small attendance) and Jeff had a Bloody Mary. In a way, good drinks and good music and writing, as far as I am concerned, come mostly in small editions, without crowds, in intimate settings.

The set started with the two saxophones exchanging fire. James Carter would toss out a melody with a light Mozartian touch, and David would dig into it, with fewer notes more painfully targeted, the way Clapton could in rock hit a good note that hurts, but even more soulfully and jarringly. That established the tone for the whole set as a playful duel between the young technician, whom Winton Marsalis discovered and ushered into the music scene, and the old bluesy jazzist, who had played with Amiri Baraka and recorded more than two hundred CDs. David looked old to me, so I was disconcerted to find out that he was a year younger than I, only forty-five. Still, to me he looked like he was sixty, had almost a homeless look about him, like someone who could play in the subway passages with a hat out for quarters. The more the evening progressed, the faster he played, and in his eagerness he stood on tiptoe and shuffled his feet so much that it seemed he was tap-dancing. His whole body was projecting and blowing into the saxophone and his spittle flew out of his instrument from a hole in the front, and in the cross-shafts of stage light, it sparkled together with sweat that burst out from his forehead like sparkle-fire from a Christmas tree. There is something special about playing wind instruments—the melody comes right out of your lungs, out of your soul. Sure, you finger it, but the breath you give to the song leaves you airy and dizzy, and even if the musicians do not take drugs, they get into an amazing breathless ozone layer of swooning ecstasy. After the slow parts, and the sadness, they arose into total abandon in the fast exchange of all they had in them. In parts, James and David played in tandem, to augment the melody, and then they would depart each his way, and one would break out into a solo while the other gave him counterpoints and question mark sounds, as though there was an interview going on, and finally the soloist would depart into an improvisation on his own, while the other player would be on the side panting like a dog. The stoned drummer and the organist had their parts, naturally. The organist covered for the absence of the bass, but with many low tones from the bass saxophone and the organ, the absence wasn't a vacuum. Nobody sang, but the musicians did hum and groan, and James had the habit of breaking off his solo with a loud sigh—Ahh—in a descending tone.

When they were done, after an hour and a half, they were done. No amount of clapping could get them to play more. It was clear they had given up their ghosts, and now they sat, dazed and emptied, and slowly they walked upstairs to recover.

Jeff and I followed to talk with them. I introduced myself to David, and he said, Where you from? And I replied, I am a mass murderer from the Balkans.

I like that, he said. The drummer and the organist said, That's great, that's a catchy intro. Jeff said, He's just kidding you, he's a writing fellow at the New York Public Library with me.

David wanted to know what we wrote, and insisted that we come back tomorrow to give him our books. Now you cats don't forget to do that, will you?

Perhaps I would not have forgotten to do it, but I missed the last express A to Inwood, upper Manhattan, and so I took the number 1, thinking it would be faster than the A local. The A is fine because even if you fall asleep on it, you wake up at the last stop and you don't have to worry about stops. Then you simply get out. On the 1, I fell asleep and woke up in the Bronx, way up at 243rd Street. I walked so slowly over to the other side of the tracks that I missed a train, and waited for more than half an hour for the next one to get home—and I got home at two in the morning, walking past dealers, whores, and adolescents who played basketball in the street. The following day, I didn't have enough time to go back to the club—I had to pack since my stay in New York was over, on a good note. Maybe it was a little too much in the measure of 9/11, but after all, that gave us a strange quick tempo to live up to. The tap dancing David blowing out his soul and his ghost through the bass saxophone certainly did play in that frenzied measure.

THE ART OF COUGHING

COUGHING CAN BE SERIOUS BUSINESS, but usually it appears to be non-profit, especially with dry coughs. As a kid (in Daruvar, Croatia), I was an avid cougher, but the gravity of the attention I was getting irked me, and so I attempted to turn coughing into a silly enterprise. A friend of mine and I, while we had chronic bronchitis when we were both around twelve, competed in the loudness of coughing.

At the beginning of the winter, I had wanted to deny that my bronchitis was full-fledged again, so I suppressed my cough. I tried to breathe soundlessly, but occasionally a rumble voiced itself in my throat and I wheezed. At night I coughed through the pillow to muffle the sound. I grew tired of hiding the cough and of being ashamed of it; not only did I cough freely afterward, I added as much volume and sound to my cough as I could to sound impressive. My friend Damir did likewise; by our explosive coughs we could recognize each other's presence from the opposite ends of our huge school, a palace which had belonged to Count Jankovics in the nineteenth century—a massive building with walls four feet thick. The dark attic allowed cylindrical shafts of dust, haze and sunshine to spread through many oval windows—holes for cannons. The dank basement hid a winery, with mostly white wines in large oak barrels. Our education took place with wine fumes rising through the floorboards (you can't question the sound foundation of our knowledge).

Damir and I hacked. We expectorated rasping sounds from our lungs and throats; now that was a different art from plain coughing. Here, you strictly controlled the rough sound, letting it vibrate deep in the throat. Without good bronchitis, you can't do it. The bronchitis gave us low sounds as though our voices had mutated into sonorous masculine basses. We roared from the opposite ends of the school corridors. Now, several thugs from higher grades didn't like our civilized game, and they knuckled Damir on the head, which didn't prevent him from proudly hacking again. They never bothered me since I had an undeserved reputation of being a thug myself. Or perhaps the thugs had tacitly declared him a winner of our contest for loudness, and that was his reward, while my hacking wasn't loud enough to elicit recognition and (dis)respect. Actually, it was loud, and it hurt my already sore throat, but I didn't want to lose even if that meant bleeding.

Damir bassooned from acoustically sound spots. He'd stand on the stairway descending into the town and announce his illness haughtily, as though to say, I can be sicker than any of you, and I like it, unlike you timid people who rush to doctors. Hearing him from the town center, three blocks away, while he roostered like that, was possible only when we were snowed under. Not that many cars drove in the town at that time, but enough, and mostly loud ones, hacking in their ways and emitting diesel clouds, so that you couldn't hear shouts from the opposite side of the street. When snow covered Daruvar, peasants, who were usually chased off the roads by city-slicker cars, rode in horse-pulled sleds, and they used bells to make sure not to run you over. One old man in particular liked to ride on snowy days with his mules. He couldn't afford real horses. Nevertheless, he proudly cracked his whip over the mules' heads but never hit their hides. With his white beard and red face he looked like a gaunt Santa out of employment; Santa who had never tasted salmon. I hitched to his cart and sledded on a tray. For some reason, the old man counted as one of the town fools, and we kids loved our fools and followed them all around, in the hopes of hearing and seeing something hilariously odd. I think this old man, Kovacevic, had an aura of total independence and originality, which made him strikingly attractive to boys. Probably in the States such a following of boys would be inadmissible for the simplistic interpretation that there was a pedophile in question. The old man actually guarded himself against boys, who would sometimes out of sheer cruelty throw iced snowballs at him. Later on, since he grew deaf and still lived in his old-world mind, he walked across the road, and a truck killed him. Anyway, when the old man wasn't cracking his whip and ringing, and Damir did his bit, I heard him. He had driven his bronchitis to new heights, to performance art.

Aside from such contests and the uses to which we put the acquired skill at home (to persuade our parents to allow us to skip school and stay in bed drinking tea with honey and reading westerns), bronchitis was not fun. Coughing hard for nearly half an hour at a time produced sweat even though I had no fever; I would sweat from the sheer labor of coughing, and since the fire would die in the Dutch stove before dawn, I would shiver from being sweaty in a chilly room, so it felt as though I had a high fever. In a renewed bout of coughing, with my eyes closed, I would see light pricks, a simulation of the heavenly firmament, and at points it seemed to me that if I went on, I would see celestial spaces chronically, for good. And on rare occasions, I did have a fever.

Yet, during the day, when there was enough heat, coughing made me feel good, alert, and once the big bouts were over, I wondered why people fussed about it. Bronchitis was not an illness, as far as I was concerned. I was used to it, and I knew how to deal with it, the way I had got used to dental pain. I had a bad dentist, who required numerous visits even to make one filling. First she drilled, then put medicine in and a temporary filling to cure the tooth, and on and on that would drag, and I got used to the administration of pain and wondered why people made a big deal about going to a dentist. And that they fussed and gave me thermometers when I coughed, and sometimes even took me to get an X-ray, seemed to be absurd. Of course, it was my fault that they took me to the hospital for an examination. Namely, though I had no fever, I stuck the thermometer into tea until it read a respectable 41 degrees Celsius, just to make sure to get a day off from school. I had no idea how worrisome this combination of cough and fever was to my family.

My brother, who was a doctor, took me to a hospital. He was going there anyhow, he said. In the courtyard, we passed by a fenced-off section where a dozen extremely thin men strolled listlessly. Some of them spat, others coughed. It was not an impressive cough, nothing hale and vigorous like Damir's, but a muffled, reluctant, exhausted cough. The men wore striped pajamas and slippers. The sight of them, and their sunken inflamed eyes, terrified me. What's wrong with them? I asked my brother.

Oh, they are TB sufferers.

Will they die?

By the look of them, some of them will. Most will pull through, though.

Since the hospital was saving money, the X-rays were not printed on film, but done on sight. The radiologist was not satisfied with one look. So he took another, and another, pushing me back against the chilly board, and darkening the room. I had an impression of pain in my chest after three rounds of prolonged radiation. The radiologist said the lungs

looked all right, some scar tissue was visible, but nothing to
worry about.

Naturally, at the hospital I had no fever, so we went back home.
Scars from what? I asked my brother.

Some people just have those, and they mean nothing. It's natural.

We passed by the feeble men. I wondered why there weren't
any women or children, and I asked, Do only men get TB?

No, anybody can.

No matter how much I coughed now, this was the only trip I
could get out of it, to the hospital and back. I remembered that
several years back, when my father was alive, coughing could
be more productive. Then I did have fevers, nightmares. In
the middle of one night I screamed out, *Bonica*. I pronounced
Bolnica (hospital) like a toddler would. When the members
of the family awoke, they laughed at my pronunciation of the
hospital. But after that winter and spring, when my cough
subsided a little but didn't go away, my father took me into
the Julian Alps, the southern Alps in Slovenia, to expose me to
clean air. He gave a few colorful bank notes to the hosts, and
after drinking tea with them, told me to get well and walked
to the train station. The ease with which he left me there
reassured me.

I didn't know people could be so jovial and relaxed. My
hosts sang, went to dances, harvested, and I followed them.
They took me to hike in the mountains, pick rose-hip tea,
feed goats. They never seemed to quarrel, and there was no
tension in the house. Once I walked into the bedroom when
the daughter, who was about twenty, stood naked in front of
the mirror. She was not embarrassed, yet she walked behind
the mirror and then laughed at me. I was fascinated.

My cough went away, but one afternoon, the day before my
father would arrive, I played with the outdoor tap water. We had
no tap water at our house, and hardly anybody at the time did,
so for me this was an irresistible novelty. I squirted, trying to

get the neighborhood boys, but most of the water sprinkled over me. I was embarrassed that my hosts might see me so drenched. I hid in a haystack to sunbathe. But the sun quickly went away and a cold wind blew. Yet, though the hosts called for me, I kept hiding. I liked the idea of not being findable, but when the chills became too much, I walked into the house and sat by the fire. The hosts had searched all over the village for me. The following day, my father arrived to pick me up. The hosts told him how wonderfully I had spent the summer, without coughing, and I wanted to agree, so I held my breath, which grew scratchier and scratchier, to burst into a paroxysm of coughing.

My father was upset. He could barely talk on the way back in the train. I saw that my coughing displeased him, and I tried to muffle it, but that drove it only to a greater intensity. Nevertheless, this was the first and the best vacation in my life, because of which perhaps I became an ardent traveler later on. The following summer, my father, not abandoning his project to get the cough out of me, took me to the Adriatic coast, where I learned how to swim, but I loved the cold water too much, and at the end of the summer I still coughed vigorously.

Afterward, when I enrolled at school, on several occasions my teacher interrupted her lectures and stared at me. My God, you look so thin! Stand up!

I did.

You've got to eat more.

I eat plenty, I said.

But look at you, you are a stick! You have TB?

No, Comrade Teacher, I am fine.

How can you be fine? Just look at you.

OK, look at me, I said. So?

Don't be brazen now, I am just trying to help you.

I sat down, angry. What kind of help was that? I felt strong and combative, and so I constantly fought other boys and grew good at it.

Anyway, my chronic bronchitis lasted until I was about fifteen. Then it went away, and I had a whole winter without it.

At a school routine examination, a TB test, I didn't mind getting pricked in the left arm. I took pride in pain management. However, the forearm began to itch quickly afterward, and it swelled. Several hours later I had an island, a little hill, of pus with a plug half an inch or more in diameter.

What the hell does this mean? I asked my brother.

It's a good thing. It means you have lots of TB antibodies. In other words, you can't have TB because you have lots of white blood cells specializing in the defense against it.

I left it at that. I failed to put two and two together—that I had had TB when I was six, and that, although I recovered from it, I had not completely recovered, but was on the verge of relapsing for quite a while even though I was not contagious, or at least I imagine I was not. My bronchitis, I understood later, with the games I played: exaggerating my cough, pretending to have a fever, gave my father anxiety attacks. Two of my siblings had died before I was born, one at the age of four, one at the age of one, one from meningitis, another possibly from TB. (Two siblings of mine before the ones who died grew up fine, as did the three of us afterward, five out of seven survivors.) If I had put all that together, I would not have simulated high fever to get a day off from school. My family hid the fact of TB from me. I think they didn't want anybody in the town to know. People were terrified of the disease in the old style as though it were plague. If my playmates knew that I had TB, they would not have been allowed to play with me. People would have imagined that we were dirty. My father's business, making and selling wooden shoes, could have suffered. So it's great that they kept it a secret in the little town in which people sought ways to isolate individuals and ostracize them. We were ostracized enough for being Baptists.

But maybe it is because we were Baptists that they did not mention to me that I had weakened lungs. They relied on the strict sectarians and God to keep me away from smoking, which we considered a sin on the same level as drunkenness. And strangely enough, I did not develop a taste for smoking. I tried it, and was repulsed by it, despite the peer pressure; everybody seemed to smoke and enjoyed being cool, but for me, the smoke only meant irritation, choking, stung eyes, unpleasantly burnt bronchi.

My brother later confirmed that both my sister and I had TB one year, but that it was caught at an early stage, at which streptomycin was effective. I remember many nights of coughing, sweating, injections, shivering, glued eyelids. Sometimes my coughing gagged me. It seems to me I should remember more. I was old enough not to let the experience dissolve into vagueness, or maybe I wanted it to dissolve, who knows? My mind certainly successfully neglected the memories, but my lungs didn't. They asked to throw out anything suspicious, and even if there was nothing suspicious in them, they went into systematic cleaning campaigns, blasting through the bronchi and potential intruders. Sometimes I felt perfectly fine, or even excellent, yet there would be this cough, perhaps not even bronchitis, but simply a habit I couldn't quit. So as I coughed with Damir and competed, feeling exceedingly silly and delightfully superficial, I had no idea that beneath the surface of the silliness hid something serious. I was successfully kept in ignorance, free to irritate and worry all those around me with my obnoxious tendency to indulge in the coughing pastime.

Now, thanks to modern medicine, this is a short essay; otherwise, it would perhaps be longer, or perhaps it wouldn't be at all since I would not have lived to write it. I am done with the disease, except to think of it vaguely. What luxury. At least that is what I hope. Recently, however, I read in a book about TB that childhood tuberculosis can recur in old age when the immune system is seriously debilitated. Not that I want to imagine it, but the thought does visit me that if I get extremely weakened, I can guess what will get me. Especially now, it's clear that the bacillus can mutate, and there are strains of it that are multi-drug resistant. Modern medicine has conquered the disease for the time being, but medicine has been around barely a couple of millennia, and we as a species, depending on how we look at ourselves, around a million years at best, and the bacillus may be as old as three billion years. So, who is the better survivor? Well, this comparative question makes me clear my throat.

ON SLEEPING

MOST PEOPLE ARE FAR MORE adventurous in their waking state than in sleep, but I belong to the approximately ten percent of the population whose behavior in sleep is riskier than in wakefulness. In sleep, I go through phases of drowning, murder, or near murder, and I risk heart attack probably more than someone having a party on cocaine. Actually, I was at war with bad and loud sleepers until I discovered I was one myself.

Late one night in a graduate student dorm, I was hitting my sleeping roommate with a tennis racket. I had been barely awake myself. Every night his explosive snoring kept me awake. He woke up and screamed. He was furious and though I apologized, I was, too.

But then a strange thing happened. He was waking me up by the same method. I have news for you, buddy; your snoring has kept me awake for hours.

In the morning we were both miserable and tired and he recommended that we jog, but neither of us could do more than three circles around the Longhorn Stadium. I blamed it on his keeping me up, but when he was gone for the weekend, I kept waking up tired. In fact, all my life I had been a poor sleeper, and a terrible grouch in the morning. I simply took that as a temperamental trait, until one night after wine tasting in

San Luis Obispo. I woke up unable to draw a breath. My heart beat wildly. Electrical shock waves were coursing through my tingling body. I tried to move and I couldn't. I saw blue light although I was sure there was no light in the room.

What the hell is going on? I thought. Am I dying? Heart attack? Stroke? When I managed to inhale, I almost asphyxiated because a gagging reflex was triggered by my stuck throat.

I got up, gasping, and I felt fortunate to be alive.

My heart beat arrhythmically in the morning, and my hosts, freaky Californian health fanatics who ate everything with flax-seed oil, looked at me, and said, My God, you look terrible.

My arrhythmia went on for a couple of days. I attributed that to the chemicals in the red wines but still, it was excessive, so I went to see my doctor, who, because of my family history of heart attacks, immediately ordered isotope and sonogram tests of my heart. To my surprise, my heart tested all right and my arrhythmia went away. My doctor was puzzled, and he wanted me to kick the only habit I could never kick: coffee. In the morning, waking up groggy and grouchy, I can clear my head, or at least attempt to, with coffee best of all. A friend of mine worked in a sleep clinic and when I described to her what was going on, she suggested that I undergo a test at the clinic. My head and body were all wired to EKG and other monitoring machines. Naturally, I slept badly. Who could sleep well with sticky tapes pulling hairs all over your body?

The test result was that I stopped breathing up to forty times an hour, and up to a minute at a time: Obstructive sleep apnea, borderline severe. I was asked to answer questions such as whether I felt fresh upon waking up, what my dreams were like, and so on. I told the sleep clinic doctor that I had a dream I was drowning and trying to come up to the surface for some air. He said, That's the most typical sleep apnea dream. You probably have many nightmares every night.

Doesn't everybody?

No.

That puzzled me—how could you live without nightmares? What kind of life is that?

He gave me a continuous positive air pressure machine. Now the air was blasted into my throat, through my nose, and if my tongue by any chance collapsed into the air passage, the air pressure would blast through.

So, for the first time in my life, I could breathe in sleep for more than a few minutes without quitting. The air felt cool, liquid, and I had the sensation that I was drinking it. Life would be good from now on. I would be more alert, more intelligent, I would write more, I would be thinner, I wouldn't need to sleep much.

At first I slept only four hours a night that way, and felt fresher than after sleeping nine hours left to my own devices. But putting the mask cup over my nose, strapping it across my face to the back of my head, was uncomfortable, especially when I traveled. I needed an extra laptop suitcase for the machine, and at every border crossing the police would puzzle over what this was. In the morning, I would have lines cutting across my face where the strap had been, and my forehead skin would be scrunched up.

Another problem was that with the sound the machine made, I scared my little children, son and daughter, who were about seven and three. With the tube hooked up to my face over a mask, I looked like a space alien. My wife didn't like the look and the sound of it either, and they liked it even less when I occasionally got drunk and slept without the machine, snoring and snorting like a monster, even worse than previous to using my machine, and so I was kicked out of the house to sleep on my own in my studio.

Now, I have found out that nearly everybody has his medical hazards and that these are a great cause for fraternizing. I have made friends with a writer, Bob, through discovering that he had sleep apnea, too. We were having breakfast in St. Petersburg, Russia, and I saw lines running across his cheeks. He looked like a football player, with a big rib cage, a frequent adaptive technique the body uses to fight with oxygen insufficiency—the body builds you extra large lungs. So, seeing the lines, I said, You have apnea, don't you? Soon we were exchanging anecdotes about sleep and sleeplessness. He occasionally stopped breathing for two minutes at a time, and he couldn't be without the machine.

For me, the effect of using the machine wore off. I didn't like all that strapping. I thought I would learn how to sleep on my belly if necessary, but no monstrous machines for me. After two years of using it, I quit. Apparently, that's the most usual course of using the machine.

You could also have a dental device placed into your mouth, to make your lower jaw protrude forward, which would create more space in your throat. I tried that—it was so tight that it felt like it was crunching my teeth. Actually, it did crack one of my teeth and its bed in the maxillary bone, which had to be rebuilt after a surgery. Although I was already an American citizen, I didn't sue the dentist. I realize that's not very patriotic of me. For revenge, I simply imagine that the dentist has accumulated enough bad karma.

I suppose the oral device could be done better. Or you could go the surgery route. Either have your nose knocked into shape or part of your throat cut out. I visited a surgeon, and he claimed that surgery wouldn't do much good. My tongue was too thick and loose—I was a very reticent child, who knows, maybe I failed to develop the muscle—and it worked as a plug. If I had laser surgery to make it thinner, I would bleed quite a bit, and then, the tongue tissue would regenerate itself within two years, and I'd be back at square one. It was not worth it according to him. My nose didn't deviate enough to be considered a cause but merely a contributing factor. Weight?

He claimed it was pretty normal. Should I become as thin as a yogi? He didn't think that would eliminate the cause of the apnea. My tongue would be the last to get thin, and the same mechanics would be taking place. My niece, a nose and throat specialist in Croatia, thought that he wasn't right—that if I became extra thin, I would be all right. Yes, but how do you do that when you have an energy crisis every day? The energy crisis leads you to eat and to drink. OK, like most Americans, now I have cause to diet and exercise, and maybe that will lead somewhere (like less exercise and more weight). I read up on research. Some antidepressants apparently ease sleep apnea. Now, I don't trust that. Our pharmacological companies, our legal drug pushers, are so aggressive, that I don't want to yield to their tricks. For the time being, you know what? I like my nightmares. I think I wrote better a couple of years ago when I wasn't using the machine and had lots of nightmares. The thing about apnea is that it keeps you dangling in that zone between wakefulness and sleep, where you dream. Sure, you go without the deep sleep and you might go insane from that, but at the same time, your mind is constantly blasted with nightmares, which may be a good pattern for the day and imagination. I wouldn't be surprised if apnea turned out to be a particularly artistic disease. Balzac by all the symptoms—big chest, severe coffee addiction, peculiar sleep hours, great appetite, heart attack—must have had sleep apnea, and so did probably Beethoven and Brahms. I'm not sure at the moment whether my own medical hazard, apnea, is so much part of me that I need it, or whether I should try once again to eliminate it. I'm writing this at 1:45 am, having woken up, so this is a sort of dream I have, that apnea is good for me. Even the dream I had before waking up, a thousand rattlesnakes advancing upon me, was probably the consequence of the rattle my throat made, but it was so vivid that I don't need to see a movie.

FRIENDSHIP ADDICTION

"Friends? Who needs them?" said a Korean friend of mine. "I don't make friends. I have a wife and a child, that's enough social life for me."

I was surprised by his attitude but the more we talked about it, the more it made sense. Friends eat up your time, make you self-indulgent, exert peer pressure from early on, so you won't succeed in work. I know many people who flunked out of school thanks to spending time among friends. A friend of mine in Belgrade had a choice once, to play a game of chess with another friend, or to go to the final exams in the school of architecture. He was ready for the exams, but on the whim of a moment, he decided to play chess, and he didn't show up for the exams, and so he flunked.

Many people start smoking and develop other bad habits because of hanging out with their friends. When I am around friends, I tend to drink too much. In fact, right now, while writing this essay, I have a headache because I drank too much wine with my Russian friend Misha last night. Now I wish I hadn't stopped by in Albany to see him. He even brought out Cuban cigars, so we could hurt our lungs, for old times', friendship's sake.

I know friends who have stolen each other's girlfriends and run off with them. I still think a childhood friend of mine stole my father's Swiss watch, my only patrimony.

If friendships tend to be so bad for us, why do we have them? Right now I think I'd be better off without friends. I would be writing a novel this minute but because of friends, I have a complaint, and I am laying it out here.

If something is bad for you but you keep doing it, it's a habit, and if you know it's a habit and try to get rid of it but fail, it's an addiction. I am addicted to friendships. That is almost the only explanation I have.

Well, I'm not quite serious about trying to quit friendships. I like them too much. That's the stage of addiction where there's no way of quitting since the will is not there. I can't will not to have friendships; I like them, and enjoy them, and when I don't spend time with my friends, I become restless, I think of giving them a call or emailing them. Still, what are friends for? You can do anything you can think of better with someone else. You can work better with a colleague. You can confess to your priest or psychologist better, without having to feel embarrassed or ashamed. You can be more intimate with your spouse or partner. You can fight better with an enemy.

In terms of personal development, sure, friendships play a role. You go out into the streets and learn how to run with the pack. You figure things out, learn your relative strengths and weaknesses. You get to know who you are, what you like, and who likes you.

Friendship was good and important in my childhood when I needed to figure things out for myself and establish an identity and a sense of who I wanted to be. I was caught between the crossfire of the atheist school and a Baptist church and family. Both had a prescription for how I was supposed to think and behave. On most points, they actually agreed. I was supposed to be clean, have short hair, talk modestly, listen and obey, never fight. Consequently, I was slovenly, grew long hair, and fought every day. I fought even with my friends, just to figure out who was stronger and to what extent, and whether there was a way to become more skilled as a fighter.

As a kid, I could practice honesty and equality with friends, moreso than with my brothers and sisters. My brother was two years older than me, so there was no equality there. He was stronger, and we fought almost every day, and while I grew more and more difficult for him to beat, he stayed stronger in our early years. He could ski better. I found areas where I could beat him, such as chess, but overall, he was above me in age and in social status, from what I could tell. He had his friends, and I wasn't allowed to be with them because I was too young. At one time, I almost killed him, which improved our relationship almost to the point of friendship as he quit bullying me as a pastime. Once, when he was threatening me, I picked up what at first I thought was a stone, but it turned out to be a chunk of rusty iron, half the size of a grenade. When he didn't heed my counter-threat—One more step and I will throw this at your head!—I threw the iron ball, struck him right below the hairline on the forehead. He went out cold and had to be taken to the hospital, and to this day he has a scar.

I made a friend on my own. A boy named Ljubo moved to our neighborhood, and we examined each other over the fence. I'm stronger than you, I said. No, I'm stronger, he said. I jumped the fence and we wrestled. It turned out I was stronger but he could do many things better than I, such as catch frogs and snakes with his bare hands. Anyhow, there was a sensation of equality, and I could tell him anything on my mind and he told me anything on his mind, such as which girls we liked. We compared notes on our development. I could talk to him about things I couldn't mention to my brother or my mother.

Visiting my friend also gave me a glimpse of another world. My family was strictly religious, Baptists, and his, Serbian

Orthodox, wasn't. In his yard, I watched plum brandy being distilled, parents drinking.

My friend gave me an opportunity to be bad, that is, free. When we were eleven, we walked into his father's room. He collected the one-ounce bottles of various whiskeys and brandies. We tasted them, and though we hated the scorching taste, we challenged each other to see who could drink more. In a week we emptied his father's collection, but so we wouldn't get caught, we filled the bottles with our urine. We admired how similar the urine looked to Johnny Walker, and we were sure we wouldn't get caught. The father, Ljubo claimed, kept those just to look at, not to drink. Well, he was wrong. The father found out our misdeed in a painful way, both for him and for my friend, who got a solid beating.

We also smoked for the first time together. He stole a pack of cigarettes from his mother, and not to be worsted, I stole a pack from a hotel. We hid in my attic and smoked and coughed, feeling like Indians, who smoked a peace pipe. He became addicted to smoking right after that and never quit. I perhaps would have become addicted if we hadn't gone to the coast. There we discovered a nude beach, and for three weeks, we visited it every day. I found the naked bodies of adult women so fascinating that I forgot to smoke a single cigarette the whole vacation, and after it, I found that I had lost the smoking habit.

When he moved to another end of our town, our friendship diminished, and I made other friends. I moved to the States, and he stayed home. During the Serbo-Croatian war, he became a Serbian soldier, and I heard reports that he participated in the bombing of our hometown. That friendship seems to be ruined; it is hard to forgive something like that—anyhow, it will take a couple of decades perhaps. On the other hand, maybe the rumor is not true. And maybe I made his childhood bitter, who knows; maybe it was partly because of me that he resented the town.

I made an unusual friend whom I respected. He was physically relatively weak and suffered from scoliosis but he was tremendously intelligent. Darko (not his real name) got a telescope and invited me to see the sky from his rooftop. He dazzled me with his astro-knowledge. He also excelled in courage—he drove a motorbike without a license in daredevil style. And he read Dostoyevski and Nietzsche. We argued about Christianity, Hinduism, Marxism and all sorts of things. His conversation was stimulating, if sometimes overly rhetorical and pushy. Many people found him intimidating intellectually. He played the piano, and won the Yugoslav competition for conservatory students of the piano by playing Tchaikovski's *First Piano Concerto*.

At the time, I planned to go to medical school to become a psychiatrist. I was also tempted by philosophy. There was a bit of competition between us, and although he was much more successful than I was so early on, he always treated me with respect. My going to the States to study, he said, gave him courage to do likewise. He came to the New England Conservatory of Music. I visited him in Boston several times and he visited me in New York.

In some things he was a late bloomer, intentionally so, even claiming that sexuality was terrible for spirituality. So, while visiting me in New Haven, when my girlfriend moaned at night with me in bed, he, as a good guest, got worried, so he brought her water with aspirin, and only when he saw us scrambling for covers did he understand the nature of her pain.

Later, he had a playboy stage, working as an accompanist for the Boston Ballet Company. When I visited him there, he grinned from ear to ear, surrounded by ballerinas, more pretty women than would ever surround me, and he dated some of them. We got married around the same time, and have children about the same age. Well, his son is one year older than mine, and my daughter is one year younger than his younger son. Now the competition has transferred to our kids.

His kids have been trained in the piano and cello just like my son. My son enjoys playing Bach suites; occasionally, I remember Darko talking about celestial harmonies and Bach. And his kids excel at languages, just the way I did. Darko has become religious and he practices various forms of mysticism, something I tried to do in my adolescence. I cannot claim that I have crucially influenced him but together with my older brother I have played a significant catalytic role. And he has done likewise for me. I have not become a psychiatrist, but a writer, a composer of words, something similar to being a musician. Actually, I cannot ascribe to his influence my bad choice of career.

Although we competed in many ways, he wasn't the mean kind of friend who would talk badly behind your back. He read some of my stories and claimed that he liked them and praised them to others. Now, that was something unique because I had some other friends who, when they read my stories, looked only for weaknesses and reflections of American corruption and simple-mindedness. So Darko proved to be a genuine friend, rejoicing in his other friends' excellence and achievement. One thing about him, he was a Serb but managed to stay in Croatia and keep his job during the nationalistic regime. Even amidst the war, our friendship didn't waver. I could tell that his sympathies were with Belgrade certainly more than mine were, but we managed to overcome our differences through a sense of humor, irony, and satire. We shook our heads at the overall stupidity of the wars and nationalism, and proceeded to play music and read stories. He wrote, too, several reviews of the contemporary music scene, and I admired those. I could tell that he had the attitude, I could do what you do if I chose to.

Friendship helps us gauge where we stand. It reminds us of our earlier promises, and gives us continuity. We calibrate our performance in many areas and even overall through how we are seen by friends, and by how we see them. Each time I visit Darko after an absence, he gives me a summary of his life, his achievements, his philosophy, even the material state of affairs, such as how many apartments he possesses, and how many miles his Mazda has accumulated. He goes overboard that way, so on the last occasion, he talked for hours about himself. He got a black belt in karate, he could swim that far, he could lift so much weight. Now that was truly wonderful—through discipline and exercise, he had overcome his childhood scoliosis, and now had the athletic body of a twenty year old. When we got out and met a well-known Croatian writer together, Darko recounted his physical success story, and wanted us both to feel how big and hard his biceps were. That was simple and charming and impressive. He had worked hard to get to this point, starting as a sickly boy and now in his middle age he was a healthy and strong man.

But he kept going, and talked all evening about himself.

He gave me newspaper reviews of his piano performances in Austria and Italy. He talked about renovating his apartment on the coast.

Finally, I managed to squeeze in a word, a question, Well, don't you want to know what I am up to?

Sure, go ahead, shoot.

I've just got a two-book deal with HarperCollins, with foreign rights sold in several countries.

Wow, he said.

At first he seemed happy, but then he sank into silence and depression for most of the evening, and he talked about what a failure it was to stay in Croatia, how limited the country was, how a CD he made there had no chance of seeing the world, how it was only local, and how even locally, classical music was dead, and so what's the point? I'm sure he'll get over it all, and we'll be friends as before, although it appears that the friendship has to be a balancing act of commensurate achievement. I don't think my achievement is any better than his—it's different. Still, it felt as though we had played a tennis match and I carried the day, and I must say, I did get some satisfaction from that. On the other hand, I hoped I hadn't set up the stage for another evening of his talking too much when I visit Croatia next time.

In the meanwhile, Darko and I admired a friend of ours, whom neither of us had seen in a while because he'd become more successful than we. He was a minister in Croatia, and now had become an ambassador to Russia. When I saw Kovacevic last, he had just become a minister, and unlike before, when he retold many jokes and scintillated with brilliant expressions of thoughts, he was now slower, more self-assured, almost bored. He clearly didn't feel any pressure to prove anything. He used to be a writer and professor and editor, but now, it seemed, he was beyond that; his arena of play was bigger, he was a true pro. Maybe he'd become too successful for our friendship to resume. If it can't resume on approximately even footing, it can be suspended for a while. The question is always, What can we do together? If we can only talk of what we do and we do dissimilar things, and not play some game or work together, we have lost the basic groundwork for friendship.

Maybe friendship stems partly from the psychological aversion to lonesomeness. Mind detests a vacuum. There has to be another mind to communicate with dialectically, bounce ideas, improve them, have a dialogue and dialectical games. Of course, in writing, I need precisely an ability to endure lonesomeness, so when I call a friend, sometimes I shirk my work, and I feel weak. The very act of friendship puts me in the loser role. It would be perfect to be self-sufficient and to write twelve hours a day; I would be rich and famous then.

Maybe it's best simply to have a memory of friendships, and to write about them, the way Proust did, who thought that he was enjoying his friendships more intimately when writing about them than when being with the friends directly. So, strangely, I practice my Protestant guilt through indulging in a few vices— having the third glass of wine, rather than limiting myself to the sanctified second, and spending the third hour with a friend, rather than limiting the get-together to an hour or two. There's this lazy effect of lingering, of excess. Friendship is excess. You can't be friends without that potlatch of time-sacrifice; there's no such thing as instant or five-minute friendship. It's not a quickie. It's a protracted trench warfare, in which you stay in the same trench, dug up against the world and world wars; in the trench, we create an impression of independence and freedom, of an alternative to the world gone astray, precisely through our going astray. There's always that sensation of smoking cigarettes for the first time in being somehow bad and therefore independent from the world—but at the same time, dependent on the friend for all that.

I think I'm addicted to that sensation of freedom to be slightly bad—to say something provocative, to tell a bawdy joke. And of course, to get feedback on how I'm doing. I want to know that I am doing well, that I'm strong enough, clever enough. I'm addicted to that assessment aspect. What is success if your friends don't recognize it? Isn't the whole point of success this, that your friends would respect you?

But here it becomes a delicate balancing act. You don't want to be much more successful than your friends, or at any rate, to boast of it.

That your friends may not always delight in your successes I found out on several occasions. I was twenty-five when I got my first writing fellowship, ten thousand dollars, a lot of money then, in 1984. I immediately rushed off to see a friend of mine at Yale, son of an American diplomat in East Germany. He was a brilliant mathematician and pianist who loved to play Goldberg variations, and if anything, I was inferior to him in terms of achievement. Our friendship was partly predicated on my admiring his mathematical and musical genius, and I was more of a joker than he was. When I told him I got first recognition for my writing efforts, I was laughing for joy. Mark reacted with disbelief at first and then he was visibly upset. Good for you, he said, and the way he said *for you* sounded like, *but not good for me.* He began talking about himself, how he should have entered piano competitions but didn't. We didn't go out to have a beer, not that time. The timing was bad for Mark. He was graduating, and he didn't apply to pursue theoretical math or piano studies as he had planned earlier, but rather, in a bout of self-examination and practical pressures, he'd signed on for an actuarial traineeship program at Blue Cross/Blue Shield, a line of professional work which would assure him excellent income and a stable future. He had already felt that he had betrayed his talents, and there I was, coming out of left field, taking a risk by abandoning anything practical to pursue my imaginary talents and seemingly getting somewhere. I did not know we were both competing somehow. After that, my friend married, and then envied me that I wasn't married, and I began to treat him as a joker, and he admitted that he hated my humor and jokes, so we ceased to see each other. Years later, he constructed a mechanism by which he executed himself, a form of strangulation.

It seems to me that male friendship is so much predicated on the potential for comparison and competition that we end up making friends in our fields, where it's easiest to compete.

I have a friend now, Dave (a pseudonym), who is an excellent writer. He has many virtues; he tells funny anecdotes, throws good parties, and when I was dry-walling my studio he came over and helped me finish the job without wanting any compensation for that. He is a hard worker and he doesn't detest work, unlike me.

Although we are different from each other in many ways, we compete, somewhat playfully. He's thinner than me, and he pokes me in the belly to remind me that I'm losing there (gaining pounds but losing the battle). He just ran a marathon. If we go out for a beer, he likes to flirt with waitresses, meaning nothing serious; he simply perhaps wants to prove that he's more noticeable than I am; or maybe he wants to appear "bad" in a good, sporty way. I smile at this benevolently; I publish more and win more awards and fellowships. For the time being, I'm winning the writerly game (of course, that can change any day), but he wants to prove that he's winning most everything else. If we talk about literature, it turns out that he's read more and remembers more than I do. Sometimes I get tired of that, and I say, How can you read that much crap? I choose my reading more carefully.

He just got married to a woman much younger than himself, for example, and they have athletic vacations, hiking in the mountains, and so on, while I stay at home with my kids. Of course, I'd probably give him one of my books if I could be in such good shape physically as he is, and it seems to me he'd gladly put on some weight or whatever if he either had my book contracts or children the way I do.

I have bought a house in the hills in central Pennsylvania, at sixteen hundred feet above sea level. I enjoy the country. Dave has just bought a house in the Rockies, at seven thousand feet above sea level. He is literally superior to me in habitation even if it's terribly impractical for him, for, after all, he teaches in the Northeast, not Colorado. Of course, he got the house on such a high altitude not out of competition with me but out of his love of mountains and heights, which of course is a metaphor for achievement.

Some friendships are based not only on comparison but even on imitation. When I was a kid, I had a friend who imitated me. I had a girlfriend early, in sixth grade, but because of going through a religious phase and being under churchly supervision in our small town, I couldn't invite her to the movies to make the moves, and she was upset with me that I didn't progress with her, that I had no ideas about what to do other than take walks. So, while we had a quarrel, my friend talked with her and they began to go out and to the movies. I didn't want to be beaten there, so I pretended I was not interested in the girl, but for that reason, I punished my friend by beating him in ping-pong and chess, and though he was a better swimmer, I won a swimming race with him. I even out-argued him in theological arguments, or so I thought. But during it all, it seemed to me he was smug, with an attitude, Sure, you can play chess better, but so what? I got the girl. Eventually, they broke up and he went to England. Now at that time I was the best student in English at our high school, and his going to England seemed to me perhaps partly inspired by a desire to be better than me in English. Of course, there were many other things involved, and maybe it's too egocentric of me to think that. Still, when I got into writing, he outdid me in a way, by getting a Ph.D. in English literature. I never went that far. Anyhow, in our boyhood, I liked him better in another country. I was still too shy with the girl, and never got together with her. When I saw him next, she already had another boyfriend, and now we had that in common, that we weren't with her. I didn't have the need to beat him at anything anymore. I read part of his diary which he showed me, in which he wrote about the suffering some of his friendships caused him because they seemed to be based on a relentless desire to defeat him and to put him down. He made a few friendships in England, with Icelanders, who didn't seem to play by that rule of vicious competition. Even later, when we visited each other in various cities, Branko would want to prove to me that he was better than me in many things—healthier, thinner, faster, more adept with mushrooms, and so on. In New York, when I lived there for a few years after college, he visited me, and we went out. I was seeing a French woman, and we all went out for a drink. Later, she told me, What's wrong with your friend? He was playing footsie with me, and under the table he put his hand on my knee, and when you were in the bathroom he wanted my phone number and a date.

Oh, don't mind him. That's just Branko. If I have a girlfriend, he wants to have her. That's his way of trying to be better than me.

How mean! she said.

It's the simple psychopathology of early friendships. In some cases it never ends.

Friendships, however, don't only propel you to excel in competition; they can propel you to stagnate for the sake of equality. Peer pressure was based mostly on that in high school; I had to pretend that I was studying less than I was, just so I wouldn't appear to be a nerd. I spent hours talking with friends when I could have been studying, and of course I was learning how to be bad, smoking cigarettes, drinking wine on vacations (we didn't have to be eighteen to walk into a bar and order wine). The competition became: who could drink more wine and not vomit? Some of the friendships became such downward pulls that I resorted to a famous saying: With friends like these, who needs enemies? Eventually, I improved the saying: With friends, who needs enemies? Enemies keep you alert, competitive, and friendships lull you into mediocrity, and through peer pressure, keep you back and down, and eventually, down and out. Some of the most excellent friends I knew in my hometown became alcoholics, and true enough, they are fun to talk with, telling jokes and anecdotes, but they sacrificed their lives to their friendships, proving that they were fun, that they were not betraying friends by leaving hometown for large cities and countries and professions.

It seems to me that without so many friendships, I would have written more, and I'd be healthier, but then, maybe not. Who would I be trying to impress now, if not my friends, or at some level, surrogates of friends, colleagues?

Yes, it's true, I'm a male-friendship addict. Some of my friends now are too well-established and too family-oriented to have that sense of time and timelessness that hanging out with friends requires, so I have noticed lately that I make friends with younger men, sometimes a few years younger, and other times, a whole decade and even more. There's that fresh element of the joy of drinking, or the joy of anecdotes, or writerly competition, and in some ways, a sense of revisiting the past, because after all, these friendships have been fun, lively, unpredictable, one of the best parts of life. There are more mature and wiser friendships that I could have with people a bit older than me—and actually, I have a couple like that—but the immaturity and vitality of a new friendship is an enlivening and rejuvenating deal.

CARTHAGE, ALGIERS, AND FES

Ceterum censeo Carthaginem esse delendam

I WROTE THIS TRAVELOGUE on my typewriter twenty-nine years ago, and since it's not digital—although typewriters were plentifully digital—I am transcribing it on my computer and therefore it will change, and it will be introduced, and even somehow concluded. In my notes, the trip is described only until Morocco.

Anyway, this trip took place after I failed to meet with an Oxford lawyer who wanted to travel with me to Poland. His timing was perfect. We were to go into Poland on December 12, 1981, the day before martial law was instituted. He must have known something (he did confess in a drunken moment that he'd worked for the British Intelligence service, and was furious about that the morning after); as we had no cell phones at that time, and his train was delayed (and I didn't know that), we did not meet. We were to meet in a lawyer's office in Palermo. I had looked forward to the trip partly because of my friend's terrific wit. Nothing matches English eloquence and wit for a lover of the language, and I loved English at that time. Later, I found out that I had missed him by an hour.

This could have been an exciting travelogue about Soviets in Warsaw, especially if we had been detained. Perhaps I would have had something politically interesting to say, unlike here.

I went south instead, through Trapani, where I found lots of Germans and Brits smoking and sleeping on the dock, waiting for a boat to take off to Tunis after a two-week strike of Italian mariners. I went on board, talked to an American architect who was carving pipes in walnut wood and an Italian brunette, for whose attention I competed with a tall and blond Norwegian. After a while, I grew tired of the competition, and went to sleep in my sleeping bag on the floor, next to a party of Tunisian men who put ten bottles of Johnny Walker Red on the table and didn't drink but gazed at them lovingly. My alpine bag was too hot and I woke up in a puddle of my own sweat after several vivid nightmares that I was back in Yugoslavia. The Arab men clapped when I got up. Then I talked to a French couple, who were surprised to see someone from Yugoslavia traveling. They said they had seen lots of Yugoslavs who worked in France, but none seemed to travel for pleasure. They warned me against eating dog meat in Algeria. You are crazy, I said. Algerians don't eat dog.

We were landing. The Norwegian and the lascivious Italian were still talking. Once we landed, nearly blinded by the white stones of Tunis, we stood on the dock, large slabs of polished stone. He was inviting her to travel with him, and I said to her, Why not with me to Morocco? and he answered, All right, I will travel with you. We all laughed, understanding the misunderstanding. I am traveling south, to an oasis, she said. OK, so he will travel with me. Fine. I would have preferred her but I was not going to give up on Morocco, and at least I didn't feel left out. Still, I was a little puzzled; he could have traveled with her and he chose to travel with me. In a way, that was flattering. She had looked amazing and her laughter was resonant. I would have certainly preferred to travel with her, but then, maybe I wouldn't have seen much else, so I resigned myself to the fact that I would probably now have a more educational trip.

The purposes of our travel, Jan's and mine, were similar. Namely, we had none. In a loose sense it's not true: his was not to be in his home town and not to be in Sicily where he'd had an adulterous affair, and he suspected if he stayed on he'd be shot by a jealous husband. Mine was to be somewhere other than in my Croatian town and the States. Anyway, now in Tunis, we could not find any wine at first, until we found out that wine was sold only during their version of siesta, between two and three in the afternoon. We waited in front of a dark grocery store in which there was a lot of coffee, dates, flour and spices. People waited in veils. Paying for bottles of wine, they did not look into the eyes of the shopkeeper or into the eyes of their neighbors. Upon receiving the catch, they scurried into the streets.

People in passing looked at us accusingly as we carried our bottles, one apiece. Grown men giggled. What's wrong? we wondered. We learned that it was almost all right for tourists to drink in public, but natives would be jailed for the same indulgence.

Tunisian buildings, reflecting the sun, hurt our eyes even more after we were done with a bottle of wine. We had nothing to do and we decided to see the Carthage ruins. The architect on the boat had talked about how whenever he saw a new building he wondered what kind of ruins it would leave behind. He liked only the buildings that promised attractive ruins. Love of ruins for an architect, he claimed, was quite natural, at least after a long career.

The ruins were pleasant. We roamed through them. Jan was an archeology student in Heidelberg, and had taken a break from his studies to "be real." There were thousands of small fragments of pottery. No doubt, some one hundred years later, such specks would be put together accurately. I remembered that, moreover, Carthage should be destroyed and well, it was.

In the distance the Mediterranean was even bluer than the sky, with a few white clouds drooping over the horizon.

Outside the ruins, many young men were whispering, trying to sell us copper coins—Hannibal coins, they said. Jan examined some carefully and claimed they were no older than a year and made of copper soaked in acid. Some were genuine, he claimed, but not valuable because they were surprisingly common. A man tried to sell us little oil torches. Jan said, Some of them are genuine but not worth much. I decided to buy one despite the export prohibition for old artifacts. You won't be able to take them across the border, said Jan.

I saw a marble head of a woman, and asked the seller, How much?

Fifty *dinars*. (That was one hundred dollars at the time).

Not interested, I replied.

Thirty-five.

No, not interested.

Twenty-five. His face sagged with despair.

Not interested.

He stood in a spot and spat.

I continued walking.

He caught up with me a minute later and said, Fifteen.

I shrugged my shoulders.

Ten! he shouted angrily.

No.

Five! Tears flowed out of his eyes.

That's some deflation! I said.

A pack of cigarettes? he moaned.

How about one cigarette? I said.

The young man started running away and he wailed as though I had killed his favorite dog. Now I felt sorry for him and ran after him to give him two *dinars*. He gave the marble head to me, and walked away, still weeping.

Jan, that's something, I got the head at four percent of the initial price. And it could have been one percent if I'd had a pack of cigarettes. Do they always bargain so badly?

No, this is dead season, and he's just dying for a smoke. During the summer he wouldn't have gone below twenty-five, I am sure. I packed the noble-profiled Greek bust into my sleeping bag and wondered whom I could please by giving it as a present. Then I bought some genuine olive lamps. One lamp profiled a doggy-style intercourse. I bought it to give as a present in Germany to my brother-in-law, who likes dirty jokes. Later, when I gave it to him, he said he couldn't keep it at home as it was too embarrassing, and he gave it as a present to a colleague clock repairman, who displayed it in his shop proudly.

From Tunis we took a train ride to the Algerian border. We were detained at the border. The Algerians were intrigued by my Yugoslav passport and long hair, and asked me whether I was a hippie, whether I was looking for drugs. My hair was thick, curly, shoulder-length. They asked Jan the same thing (his hair was blond and long, half way down his back), but finally, Jan's diplomatic passport helped us get through. His father was a Norwegian ambassador to Germany. Hey, you never mentioned that, I said to Jan.

Why would I?

At least you said it to them.

Yes, it can be useful. It's got me out of trouble a few times.

It seems they wouldn't have let us go through otherwise.

You are right about that.

In Anaba it was late and we had no place to sleep, but not to worry—a young man on the train invited us to his home, and woke up his aging mother to cook a meal for us. The hospitality, to my mind was wonderful, but Jan had a slightly different experience. While I was given a room all to myself, he was invited to share the bed with the man from the train. He slept on the floor instead. The house was adorned with pictures of blond girls and boys and blond angels. Jan, we lucked out because you are blond, apparently.

Tell me about it, said Jan, sore from the sleepless night.

From Anaba we flew to Algiers. The tickets were amazingly cheap, some twenty USD a person. There was no security check. We simply walked onto the plane as though it was a bus, and the seats were not assigned. And this is a socialist country with lack of liberty? I marveled. Of course, airlines had already started using security checks all over the world, partly thanks to an egg-head compatriot of mine, a Croatian, Busic, who'd hijacked a plane in 1976 at JFK, and whose bomb went off at Grand Central, killing a cop. People were happy on the plane. We took off exactly on time and landed on time. Clearly, we are not in Italy, Jan commented. This is cool.

But in Algiers at the airport there was a glitch. We couldn't find our luggage. After the flight we strolled for ten minutes and got tea to drink. The luggage from our flight was rotating on the carousel but ours wasn't there. After an hour we went to a policeman and complained, and he said, Oh yes, you were not there, so we took the bags and put them here. He pointed to a door and gave us our luggage. Namely, the luggage had arrived at the same time as we deplaned and was on the carousel, instantly available, but we were too slow to get it. Our neglect. Their system was perfect. But not everything would continue that way. We couldn't find a place to stay that night.

We spent Christmas Eve in Algiers without a hotel in a cold and windy square, where my blond friend was besieged by various men, who asked for "*un petit amour dans la chambre.*" Several *clochars* were trying to change money with me. I didn't know what the black market range of exchange was. Jan was saying that as it was Friday we wouldn't be able to change any money until Sunday, so I changed a fifty dollar bill at the official rate. Later I discovered that I could have got three times as much. Ten minutes later, after my exchange, a sleek man sat next to Jan and conversed with him in French about Germany and France, and he placed his hand on Jan's thigh. Jan shouted *Finis*! I have a room with Johnny Walker in it, said the man. Why not make *amour dans la chambre?* Jan pushed his hand away again and threatened to smash his nose. The man shook his head, Why so violent? All I want to do is make peace and love.

Yes, he has a point, I said. Relax.

This is ridiculous, said Jan, and dozed off. I did too. A few minutes later I looked over: the man's little finger began to rise. Several minutes later it touched Jan's thigh ever so slightly and began its ascent. Jan woke up, he shouted, *Finis!*

Je suis désolé, said the man, and then pulled out a banknote, offering it to Jan for a bit of *amour*. I looked over and said, Wait a minute, can I see the money?

It's not fake. My friend just bought it from Swedes, said the man.

Can I see the note?

All right. The man held it before me. I saw it had the same folds as mine. My fifty dollar bill could now lay Jan. I laughed, and said, My friend, here's your chance to retrieve our money so we can change it better next time.

Go away! Jan shouted. *Pas encore!*

The man left, looking dejected, his head hung low.

Hey, Jan, look how sad he is. You could have made him happy and we'd have more money. That was not nice of you. I laughed, and added, You have a lot of integrity.

He's disgusting. I could have killed him.

We couldn't sleep, and so we walked around the city. It was a peculiar Christmas. Policemen in boots were kicking a sleeping man in the streets. He woke up and screamed and they kept kicking him. A couple of blocks away, another couple of policemen were clubbing a man.

In the morning we waited for two hours in a throng of people to get a ticket to Oran. There I ate the best oranges and bananas in my entire life. We rented a hotel room on a hill and spent two days walking. The city was full of boys playing soccer. Who knows, maybe one of them would be Zidane later on. At the time Zidane must have been five years old, in Marseilles, doing the same thing these boys were doing, playing soccer in the streets. The whole city was full of boys, and their noise, life, energy. Even then, Jan and I commented on how Europe in contrast looked like a retirement home, a museum of things past, rather than life present and to come, unlike North Africa.

Our train ride to Fes in Morocco was a long one, and beautiful. To kill the time I was reading *The Idiot* by Dostoyevski, a truly idiotic thing to do during such a potentially illuminating trip. I must confess that it's one of my least favorite Dostoyevski novels, full of apparently aimless scenes and conversations, which lack the immediacy and urgency of those in the *Brothers*, or the wit of *Notes from the Underground*, or feverishness of *Crime and Punishment*. This perhaps would have been a better read in Poland than here. We slept on the train, one night, and after a long delay at the border near Oujda, we continued to Fes, where we arrived in the evening. Once again, we couldn't find a hotel and we didn't care. We recounted to ourselves the trip digest—Jan remembered the towns we had gone through: Oran felt fine, I had good feelings there; Algiers didn't feel so good, Anaba felt good. To feel fine was a complex project. It's all about feelings, Jan said, and I am happy just to carry a feel for a place, you know?

An elderly railway worker invited us to his hut next to the train station. We sat on the dirt floor, and he said, in French, that he was offering us wonderful Moroccan tobacco to smoke. We shared a pipe. Whoa, said Jan, you will like this. He didn't tell me it was hashish. After inhaling two smokes, maybe just three minutes later, I was completely stoned, and I found everything funny and so did Jan and the old man. We sat so floored for hours, and after we had some coffee, we walked on into town. Man, after this, I need to cool off, a beer, or something, Jan said. We walked and found a bar. It was filled with men who smoked cigarettes, argued, and drank brandy and beer. Before we could order any, two bottles appeared at our table, and several men joined us, and conversed with Jan in French. One Arab man was angry, and said, No more French, why French? Let's speak Arabic. If you are tired of French, let's speak English, I suggested. Oh, English, that's even worse. I hate English. If I hear another word in English, I will smash this bottle. Go away, the others told him, and then dragged him out and threw him into the street. After a while he came back and sat by himself, frowning. A man said, I love English. We can speak in English, we can speak anything here. Yes, it's a house of Babel, said another man, in English. Jan kept conversing in his French. When we said we couldn't find a place to sleep, a man, perhaps thirty years old, said, You can sleep at my father's place. Let's go. No, they can't go, another man said, they must drink whiskey with me. We'll come back tomorrow, I said. We barely managed to leave the bar for fierce hospitality, with everybody wanting to drink with us. What a wonderful country, I said to Jan.

My father's place is two blocks away, said the man.

We walked for twenty blocks and the city lampposts disappeared.

How much farther? said Jan.

Two blocks.

But you said two blocks twenty blocks ago.

Well, yes, it's two blocks after the end of this street.

What does that mean? Jan asked. Are there blocks, or is it just the country or something?

One hundred and fifty meters. Let's go. You will like it. My father will be happy. He will roast a goat for you.

I said, Let's find out where he wants to take us, just for the hell of it. It could be an adventure.

I'd rather not, said Jan. I am not going another step into the dark. See, it's just dark there, no lights.

So what? I said. In the periphery of my hometown, it would be dark, people are frugal, they don't waste electricity.

No, man, Jan said. This doesn't feel right, let's turn back.

As you wish, I said. Let's go back to the bar and drink some more.

Our would-be host was furious. He shouted that we didn't trust him, that we were ungrateful foreigners, and called us names. He spat and continued walking into the dark.

You hurt his feelings.

Feelings. He had something up his sleeve. We are lucky we didn't go on with him, I am pretty sure—his thug friends would have probably mugged us and stolen our passports.

We walked back to the bar and in front of it, there was a huge fist fight, with a few wrestling matches, a lot of shouting, a few broken bottles.

What is going on? I asked a man I recognized.

Oh, they are fighting over your German friend.

He's Norwegian.

Some people are mad that we let you leave the bar, and I advise you, my friends, not to come back. Just keep going before they see you or else you might be in trouble. I wouldn't be surprised if someone stabbed you.

Oh? was all I offered as a comment.

So we walked gingerly and briskly away. That's something else, I said. All because of you?

I can't believe it. It's insane.

Well, you are the only blond this evening. Blonds have more fun!

Fuck, don't remind me. This is horrible. I hate it, I want to get out of this place as soon as possible.

We went back to the train station, and by the time we got there it was dawn, and we were both sober, hung over, and miserable.

Our next destination was not Casablanca as we had initially planned but Tangier. The views from the train were amazing, with the desert. In Tangier, many people tried to sell us hashish, and we engaged in shouting matches to ward them off, to convince them that we didn't want any. What didn't help our cause was that Jan suddenly changed his mind and wanted to buy some and he did and then wanted to buy more. That hash in Fes was something else, he said. I'd like to take some to Germany.

How will you get it there?

I don't know, I haven't thought it out. We'll find a spot.

Like what?

Bottom of a toothpaste tube, he said.

But they have police dogs all over the place at the border crossing.

Maybe, but dogs won't be able to smell through a layer of toothpaste and lead.

Fine, you do it, and I am not interested.

But if we take some in, visit me in Heidelberg, and we'll have a wonderful time. I know many smart girls there, and they'll like you.

Why do you say that?

You aren't blond and you come up with weird things to say. Tell you what, why don't you put hashish into your hair? It's so thick and curly, it will stay there, and the cops aren't going to think of looking through it.

Look who comes up with weird things to say. I am not transporting drugs out of Africa, I said.

Fine, be like that. But you are transporting old artifacts in your sleeping bag, and if you are caught . . .

But these are fakes.

No, actually, the bust is genuine, and so is the oil lamp. Genuine enough for jail, anyway.

But I am out of Tunis so now it doesn't matter.

We didn't talk for an hour or so. Soon we were on the boat crossing into Algeciras in Spain. I had just eaten some anchovies. The sea of Gibraltar was incredibly stormy and our ship was tossed up and down. Relieved to be in Spain, Jan and I ordered two bottles of wine and a fish meal. Once on a train to Madrid, I grew thoroughly sick. I didn't know whether it was the anchovies, or cheap Spanish wine, or the waves of Gibraltar, but I could not keep my balance. I lay on the floor and moaned. Now and then I stood up and vomited through the windows, and then lay on the floor again.

You sure know how to have a good time, Jan commented.

When we got off the train in Madrid, I noticed that the train was painted on the side, several coaches in a row, with purple streaks of my vomit. I was proud. This was some expressive art, action painting. . . How could I produce that much stuff? It seems even the drinks from Fes must have come into the mix. I felt relieved, much lighter, clearer, and literally sick of travel. Jan and I hopped on a train to Paris. Those were the days, I must say. . . we were both twenty-five, and we could go anywhere we liked, for a while. And going to Paris didn't sound all that bad. We could crash in an apartment of a friend of mine, a Jewish marine biologist who lived in an Arab neighborhood. When we arrived there, we entertained her by basically giving her the same travelogue I recounted here. I complained how Jan didn't help our cause for he wouldn't rescue the fifty-dollar bill by making *petit amour* with the well-combed Arab man.

He was disgusting, Jan reiterated.

So what, I said. If he wasn't disgusting, would the story be any different?

Maybe, he said. Yes, maybe I would have gone and fooled around with him. What, you are surprised?

Yes, well, let's have more wine. We laughed more. Soon Jan left and we exchanged a few letters over the years, but this was before the internet years, and we lost touch, and I never visited him in Heidelberg. But I lingered in Paris for a week, and saw many plays with my French friend, whose name, sorry to say, I have forgotten. Amazing to forget. We too exchanged a few letters and I lost them, and I forgot. . . and yet despite forgetfulness or because of it this is a memoir of a trip, a trip which was over by the time we reached France. Sometimes I wonder how it would have been for me if I had traveled alone, without Jan. Maybe I would have even finished *The Idiot* and would now have a higher opinion of it.

MY HUNGARY

IF I STAYED IN the same place and lived long enough in the Balkans, I would visit several countries. I heard a man, who was ninety, claim that he had been to eight different countries without ever going farther than forty kilometers from his hometown. The countries changed and came to him. I think he counted Hungary and Austria, and then the German invasion as living in Germany, the Italian invasion as living in Italy, and then the Kingdom of Serbs, Croats and Slovenes, two Yugoslavias, and then Croatia. His travelogue of going nowhere and yet being in eight countries would be fascinating and stirringly deep, no doubt, but instead, you are stuck with my more conventional travelogue of restlessness and superficiality.

As a kid, I yearned to go far, to Tierra del Fuego or New York. Hungary interested me the least as a foreign country since it was the closest, only forty miles north of my hometown Daruvar, which itself was part of Hungary for eight hundred years before World War One. If World War One had played out differently, I would have been born as a Hungarian of mixed roots, typical for the Danubian region—Croatian, Slovenian, Czech, and I am afraid, Hungarian. Daruvar means stork-town in Hungarian. Anyway, I heard that my grandparents used to speak Hungarian at home. My great-grandfather died as a lumberjack near Pecs when my grandfather was only three years old. A tree crushed him. Should that count as Hungarian roots? Poor pun, but a good question. And I was born during the Soviet crushing of the Hungarian uprising. Anyhow, the only thing that intrigued me about Hungary was the Soviet enigmatic and anti-charismatic presence. Actually, I had visited close to the Hungarian border as my brother worked as a doctor only ten miles away from it. The closer you got to the border, the more boring it became—the houses were more neglected, mortar peeled off more, there were more geese in the streets, the peasants looked gloomier and fatter, and of course, it would only get worse if I went further north, I was sure of that.

And when I got back from the States, at the age of twenty-two, the first thing I did when I was about to visit Yugoslavia was to go to Hungary from Vienna; I realized HU was a great country, and rebuked myself for not visiting it when I first went abroad. Instead, I had gone to Italy, when I was fifteen, to Trieste, where my eyes got bloodshot from car exhaust and greed. In the Budapest streets now, while looking for a place to stay, I got into a conversation with a bunch of students who invited me to play ping-pong at their dorm. A Chinese engineer won, and I came in second. Then we went out, listened to gypsy music in an ecstatic suburban tavern, and bought wine on my money, and in the morning, recalling little of the night, I was back at the train station, and my wallet, passport, everything was still sticking to my ass.

South from Budapest, the train got stuck in deep snow, and inside the train was getting progressively colder. In a compartment, while I was conversing with several people, a girl invited me to go home with her. She said it was only two kilometers away, and we would be very comfortable in her bedroom. She was remarkably beautiful, blonde and curly-haired. I said that sounded good. We trudged through the whipping snow and got to a house in a small town near Pecs. She prepared me hot red tea, gave me a glass of Tokay, and opened a jar of black caviar from Russia. Her English was poor. She said that men grew wild when they ate caviar, but to make sure I wouldn't grow wild, she would go to her part of the house. I realized her initial communication was merely a standard masterpiece of bad English; she had no intentions. She locked the glass door separating the house into two parts with a large key, undressed nonchalantly so I could see what I was missing (maybe that was intentional), and disappeared behind a huge door. I finished the jar of caviar and the bottle of yellow Tokay, and slept in a tall bed with my clothes on. In the morning the hostess walked me to the train station, we exchanged addresses; she said to write, and I said I would, but I never did. Nevertheless, my first impression of Hungary was good.

I have visited many times since, usually in transit. In 1983 I stayed for two months in the annex of a neglected synagogue, Garay utsa 48, in an apartment filled with books in Hebrew. I was trying to write on big slabs of raw paper from a shop below. I explored the city, played chess with old men in the hot baths, ate goulash in dives, and anyhow, my typewriter broke down, and I gave it to an East German mathematician in exchange for his inviting me to stay with him in Berlin for two weeks. I wrote both about Budapest and Berlin some measly twenty pages, but since I already did, I am not going to linger on that trip, but will jump to others.

I almost got into a relationship in Budapest, meeting a girl in the British library. I need a good dentist, I told her. Obviously, I had no intentions with her, but I just told her the truth. She said she knew one. She led me to a dental office and waited for me while the butcher dug into my jaw. Anyhow, my tooth did not hurt after it. And Csilla was flirty, brunette with curly hair and large swinging breasts. She had knowing eyes, a spark in them, and bright white teeth, and her father had been a diplomat. Later she visited me in Zagreb, but wouldn't sleep with me. She slid the sheets under my body and over her body so we were sheet-separated, and that is how we slept. When we were on the bus, she asked me to show her my teeth. She said, I am not going to marry you. You have had cavities. That is dangerous for the heart. I said, That is good news. I don't want to get married. Five years later, when I was in Austin, Texas, she gave me a call, and said, I am getting married in three days. Do you have anything to say? I said, I have nothing to say. And she said, That is sad. Later I thought, She still wanted us to get married? What sense did it make? It was sad we didn't get laid, true. Anyhow, out of curiosity, in 2006, twenty-three years after our teeth conversations, I visited her in Kaposvar. She lived in a large house with splendid black beams. Maybe one of these fell on my great-grandfather, contributing to my family being relatively weird. Her husband was on a trip and her daughters were there. She cooked beans, bacon, onion, and pasta. It tasted good, but I wondered why one would eat that; on my own, at home, I wouldn't eat poison like that. And she said, You look good. I visited Croatia, and so many people there were tall and healthy looking. . . You know, I have heart palpitations, there's something wrong with my heart. I didn't say anything. Of course, if you eat bacon and spend your early twenties not fucking, you will have heart problems, I was tempted to say, but then, what would be the point? She also told me she was more Croatian than I was, two of her grandparents. I said, Oh, now it makes sense. I never got along with Croatian women.

Most of my post-1983 trips to Hungary were in transit on the way to Croatia or St. Petersburg, as there were no direct flights to Zagreb from New York, and hardly any to St. Petersburg. Usually in changeovers in London, Frankfurt, and Budapest, there was too much time, and I joined—too early—the people waiting at the gates, who seemed to wilt from boredom. Not that they looked like flowers in bloom anyhow, but they still managed to wilt. Short layovers are a great solution to hectic and boring travel. I arrived in Budapest from New York at eight in the morning on my trip in 2002. Too much time to wait, and just enough time to go to the city and sight-see.

I took a minibus to the city, and had it take me to a five-star hotel—Kempinski Korvinus—because it was the most central. There, a concierge opened the minibus door for me and I evaded the hotel and walked north along the river to the parliament. As a child I collected postcards, and this building always looked most splendid to me, with so much detail, devils under the roof, no doubt, quite baroque and grand. I had five postcards with the Hungarian parliament on them. That is the thing about Budapest, since it was the center of an empire that included many peoples, and in size it was almost as large as France. I gazed up across the river to the Fish Castle. There was a palace and a castle and a cathedral of St. Stephen, but the skyline was wrinkled by the Hilton Hotel built on the old ruins. No matter how subtly that was done, there was a new structure—now that was a true empire, the Pax Americana of hoteliering, with air conditioning and ample showerheads that would chlorinate you.

I used to take the Budapest subway for two *forints* a ride in 1983. Now, twenty years later, I got a ticket, which was 106 *forints*. I wondered, why 106? Why not 100? Or 120? I didn't notice that there were machines where you could get your card stamped. I passed by a policeman, who was staring at my pocket. Perhaps he thought my wallet was strikingly fat. The subway station looked just like a Moscow peripheral Metro station, except this one was central. A controller standing at the bottom of the stairs looked—I thought she would welcome me. Which way to Deak Ter? I said, though I knew.

She: Show ticket.

I showed the pale strip of paper. I thought maybe she would puncture it.

She called over a policeman and demanded that I pay a fine, sixteen hundred *forints*. Not much money but much principle.

No, I didn't know where you cancel the ticket, I said.

You must pay the fine, Sir, she said.

Your passport, said the policeman, standing unsteadily on the big slabs of cement.

I showed the passport. When he saw it was American, he said, sixteen hundred *forints*, Mister. Standard fine.

Both of them insisted, in horrifying English, and I replied in German, You should help foreigners who get confused if you want tourism, rather than practice your old socialist tricks. All your signs are only in Hungarian. I am out of here. I tore the ticket and put it in my pocket.

I went up the escalator, and passed by another policeman upstairs. He did not react. In Russia, I got used to slotting tokens at the turnstile. In New York, I slid the ticket at the turnstile.

They could have insisted more vigorously that I pay the fine, and of course, I would have paid it. Or they could have arrested me, which would have made for a better story. But I was glad that I didn't get a better story in this encounter and that I would not be going to Deak Ter, but would roam the streets, looking for good coffee.

Each trip to Hungary contained some strange experience. I flew to Hungary for my mother's funeral in November 2006. The fare to Zagreb on short notice would have been twenty-four hundred bucks, but to Budapest it was only six hundred fifty. I went to the Alamo counter at the BP airport, but next to the counter, a Hungarian car rental representative said, You are better off renting with us. We'll give you a ride, we are only a kilometer away from the airport, and our prices are low, thirty euros a day, including insurance. Fine, I said, and I went with the man to a car rental place, which was some ten kilometers away. To rent a Skoda, the host said he'd have to run my credit card. He gave me the papers, and at first I thought that I had paid a two thousand USD deposit, in forints, but then when I reckoned more carefully, once I was on the road, I realized that I had put down twenty thousand. I was nervous about that. What if the car got stolen? I'd never get that money back. And how will I find the rental place when I come back? Was the address written anywhere? What if it turned out that they just sold cars that way. You think you are renting, and then you end up with a car, paying twice as much as it's worth? Perhaps I would have the same experience as I did with my publisher in Russia, Amphora. The editor offered me two thousand dollars for the rights to my Fiction Writer's Workshop. I said, wonderful. Can we sign now? He said, *Lusche,* next week. Then I will have the money, we will have written the contract with all the necessary clauses. A week later when I came, along Chernoia Ryechka, the building was locked. There was no activity there. A guard showed up and when I asked him whether Vadim was in, he said, No. He is gone. When is he coming back? Never. But we had an appointment! The company moved to a new building. Where is the building? Do you have the address? They are not there yet. They will continue with business in May. When I got together with the publisher's assistant, she told me that he wouldn't buy my book anyway, that they suddenly decided to change the direction, that there were too many bad writers in the world, and that a book like mine was dangerous because it would encourage more bad writers to send books, and that the best thing for them now was just to publish tested books, international best sellers and Nobel Prize winners. That's how I lost 2K—or at least didn't get the 2K. And what would happen now? What the fuck do I do with this car? Normally, I would have turned right back, but I didn't want to miss my mother's funeral. How could I? What is more important in a life than burying a mother? I was tired. The sun was terribly bright, and the traffic jam around Budapest was as bad as the approach to GW Bridge during the rush hour. I don't remember whether I had slept on the plane. I probably didn't sleep. Anyway, nothing seemed to matter. Burying my mother preoccupied my thoughts, but the discomfort of having a strange car rental kept coming up in my mind. Maybe it was a good distraction from grief.

I drove next to the river Tisza, and it looked amazingly calm, green, and the sky was hazily blue. I was tempted to feel free and elated. I would no longer need to keep visiting Croatia as I had no mother. I would no longer have to keep visiting Hungary as the transit to Croatia lost meaning. And the river view was amazingly calming, with barges, of course, barges. What the hell did they transport? Cabbage?

In Duna, a town on the Tisza River, I went to a gas station restaurant. I parked the car in the lot, using the automatic lock, and walked in. I bought a double shot of cappuccino. It was bitter, so I put in some sugar. Why do Central Europeans in general save on coffee by serving the cheapest, oldest, raunchiest mud as coffee? I looked to the other side of the room, and there stood an amazingly statuesque brunette with blue eyes, with low cut jeans, even pubic hair overflowing, flat sunburnt stomach, thin nose, full lips, and graceful hands with long fingers, which she kept moving like a pianist. Why am I noticing this? Aren't I grieving? I better not look at her, it's immoral. Not that I had any impure thoughts, I was merely struck by a sight of a beautiful woman. When she laughed, her lips revealed terrible dark teeth, some of them obviously rotten. Or were they merely smudged by coffee-mud? No, definitely rotten. Now, in the States you'd hardly ever see such a stunning looking woman, and if you did, she wouldn't have rotten teeth, most likely. I was puzzled by the paradox.

What else do I need? Water, of course, water. I bought a plastic bottle, and making sure not to look at the rotten beauty, whose melodic voice floated after me, I walked out. My car wasn't where I left it. I looked around. No gray Skoda. What the hell? Somebody already stole it? Did I lock the door? I talked to a gas attendant. He didn't understand English. He understood a little German. What is the car license plate? I have no idea, I said. What is the rental company? I completely forgot. It was a strange name, written on a paper in the car. I had a car key, but it had no information, no alarm button. I talked to another gas attendant. I was frantic. They didn't share my excitement. One of them smoked and looked bored. Probably it happened at their gas station often. Or at any rate, it was nothing unusual in Hungary. Cars changed ownership. Is there police around here? I asked. Luckily my wallet and passport were on me. The rest was nothing. It's only money. It's only twenty thousand dollars, why fret? My mother is dead. Of course, I wouldn't inherit any money, she was broke. I would need to pay two thousand dollars to share funeral expenses with my older brother. The hell with money. When you lose, you might as well just lose as much as you can, and start anew. How will I go to Croatia now? I walked around the gas station. There was a gray Skoda, much closer to the restaurant than mine, in fact right outside of it. It looked just like the one I had rented. But this one was a little bigger, and the metal wasn't as new and shiny. I came up to it and looked inside. The black jacket I had bought for the funeral was inside. I took out the key and it clicked the doors open. I sat inside, and felt a moment of joy and relief. Shit, am I losing it that badly? What got me? Sleeplessness? Now I drove south and I sped. I didn't care if I got a ticket. So what, I have the car, and what if I have to pay a fine? I could pay one hundred or two hundred, what difference did it make? But what if, in my state of zombiehood, I cause a car crash? I could run over a drunk, kill a dog. . .

Crossing the border was no problem. The trees in early November were all colorful, a bit like New England, except without the maple red. Rust and brown from oaks, yellow from beeches, lots of green from ash, but no red. New England with color theft. OK, I will not describe getting into my hometown, nor the family gathering, the funeral, etc.—I have written an essay memoir about that, much more essential than this one—but will skip to my trip back.

I found the car place easily and returned the car. They credited back the 20K, and ran the card again so I would pay two hundred ten euro, the weekly rate. They walked around the car, complained about a scratch, but then waved and went back to their cabin. Their assistant gave me a ride to the airport, and there I got a cab to the center of the city where I rented a hotel room. It was near the old fish castle. I walked down to the other side of the Danube to Pest, and I listened to some Gypsy music in a nearly desolate restaurant, and the violinist came to me and played for me. Of course, I tipped him and that encouraged him so he played more and wanted to sell me his CDs. His hair was oiled and you could see pick distances from his comb in it as thick parallel lines.

I walked in the streets. I had emailed Tibor Fischer, my writer friend, who is usually in Budapest when I visit London, and now he was in London, so there was nobody for me to visit. Strange—I had spent so much time in Budapest, but that was before internet, and I lost touch. The few people I could still be in touch with lived in different towns. No matter. I was decompressing from the funeral, and my feet, in the sneakers, enjoyed walking after being stuck in stiff black shoes, which turned out to be too narrow. Sneakers, a wonderful invention. I walked on cobbles. There were prostitutes in the streets. Not such a wonderful invention, sex for money. One, plump, in a mini-skirt that was way too short, came up to me and asked, Would you like to buy sex? No, I said. It's only one hundred and fifty euro. That's not only, I replied. I spend two hours with you. I walked down the street more, and another one, a tall brunette with rotten teeth, but not as good looking as the one from the gas station, came up and asked, Would you like a sex massage? No, I said. How much? I asked nevertheless, out of curiosity. Eighty euro, she replied. Well, that much I had, but I still said no. Now what kind of behavior would that be, coming from your mother's funeral? I kept walking, wondering whether there was jazz now in the jazz club near Vaci. No, not open yet. Now in the street I saw a truly beautiful blonde. She smiled at me. Even her teeth were great. I will not go into detail, but she also had a spark about her. This one was just friendly, she couldn't possibly be a prostitute. Would you like a relaxing massage? she asked. What does that mean? I asked. Anything you want, in all positions. That sounds interesting, I said, in all the positions. Yes, she said, top, bottom, behind. And how much? Forty euro, she said. A whole hour. We walk to your hotel, and will be good. No, thank you, I said. You want it? she said. No, I said. Why you look at me then? Well, good point, but no, can't do it. She swore in Hungarian and walked off. It seemed the better looking the prostitute, the less she charged. Why would she charge so little? Maybe she was desperate. Maybe she was a drug addict and simply needed cash right away. She had a point. It was rude of me to look at her and waste her time. I walked to the hotel up the hill. It was unusually warm and I was sweating. Maybe it was good exercise. No, it wasn't. By the time I got to the hotel I sneezed and coughed, and I shivered all night long. I was disturbed. Life was death.

In the morning, images from the funeral still kept coming back to me, such as the amazingly cold forehead of my dead mother, and the unavoidable cruelty of putting her body in the wet and cold soil, the sounds of the fistfuls of soil hitting the wood, the bees landing on the red purple carnations. . . The weather of course had been amazingly beautiful. . . just like 9/11 weather. These two events had made the idiom to *have the blues* sensible. The blue skies somehow make the misfortune appear all the more cosmic, not just locally trapped under a cloud, but expanded into the blue infinity.

I passed the airport customs, and drank the obligatory dung for coffee. An elegant girl in a miniskirt walked past me with the air of a ballerina: easy grace, effortless control of arms and legs. She sat close to me. And then a young man came over. He had got permission to cross into the zone showing his passport. The guards, two women, yielded to his pleas. He came over and kissed the girl, gazed at her soulfully, stroked her cheeks, they hugged, kissed more. He left and she walked a little, looking at the jewelry, and then came back. On the plane we sat just a few seats apart and she gave me a look which was perfectly unexpressive. The plane went to Milan, where I would change to NY. Now that is outside of the Hungarian travelogue, but I will trespass here. In Milan, I walked all around the airport, and drank fine macchiato. Even airport macchiato in Italy is better than the mud we drink elsewhere. Then I decided to get a slice of pizza and came to the counter, and there, to my surprise was the same brunette, talking to a blonde, in lively Russian. I joined the conversation, asked them what city they were from, and the brunette was from St. Petersburg and the blonde from Moscow. I know the city, I said to the brunette. I have lived there for a year. Very interesting, she said. Would you like to join us? Sure, I replied. Later I asked her, By the way, I saw you in Budapest. Your boyfriend accompanied you, and he looked devastated that you were leaving. Well, he was leaving too, going to the States. Will you see him again? Probably not. He came to Budapest to marry me. But he got only one room at the hotel, so I told him, Who do you think I am? And he said, Look, I flew all the way from America to see you and I paid for your trip. So I made him buy another room, and it was very expensive, but that must have taught him a lesson.

What lesson?

Not to draw any conclusions about us Russians. People think they can just buy us. They are lucky if we don't buy them.

And he still wants to marry you?

You saw, he is desperate. But that puts me off. And if you are curious, no, we didn't sleep together. The closest he got to sex was what you saw at the airport. In private, if he got that far, I would slap him.

That looked like very far from sex.

Konyeshna.

How cruel, I said. He paid for everything!

He felt like it. And if I liked him more, I would marry him. I have other suitors, she said.

Where?

Maybe you are my suitor?

I have enough problems.

You think you do.

Anyhow, at least that was a cheerful conversation, and to my mind it was still Hungary. Getting into an American Airlines plane, I had no sensation of going home, or leaving home, but of being contained in a metal tube for a reverse burial in the sky, for eight hours, without oxygen.

Last summer I was supposed to fly to Budapest on the way to Zagreb, but at the last minute I managed to change the ticket, so I got directly to Zagreb from London. I had a layover in London, and I emailed Tibor Fisher, who responded that he was in Budapest and that I should visit, that the city was full of. . . something or other. I forget full of what.

Do I have any conclusions about Hungary? Absolutely not. If I had visited on different days, I would have had different experiences and would be tempted to draw different conclusions. Hence, no conclusions.

VUKOVAR

15 September 1997

OVER THE PHONE, LASSEN, from Public Affairs at the UN, told Jon (a photographer friend of mine) and me that there would be no problems crossing into Vukovar. He faxed us press credentials through a photographer in Vinkovci, a town fifteen miles away from Vukovar. We drove to the UN checkpoint, past barbed wire and minefields. The guards wouldn't let us through. We needed to have a blue card, the pass they said the UNTAES offices in Vinkovci would issue for us.

We drove back to Vinkovci. A UN officer told us to go to the county office. He gave us bad directions, so it took a while to find it. What he called the main street turned out to be a narrow one, far from the center. We looked for the officer, Mr. Marek, who could issue the pass for us. However, he was on vacation in Poland for a month and a half.

Is there anybody else who can issue us the pass? I asked.

No, said a secretary. He is the only one.

I called Mr. Lassen, who said, That's incredible. With German license plates they should let you go through. They have no right to stop you.

They may have no right, I said, but they did. Could you call them up and tell them to let us through?

He promised he would.

It worked. We passed through after a brief conversation. This was the day when the transitional police force was to take over the checkpoints to Vukovar. Each checkpoint would have Croatian police, local Serb police, and UN police working together. You could tell that not much was coordinated.

At first we saw no destruction. I didn't know that we were not in Vukovar yet, but in a Serb village. Not a bullet scar on the buildings. But then, when we entered Vukovar, the picture was the worst we'd seen yet, worse than Mostar and Sarajevo. Leveled buildings, big holes in the walls from tank artillery hits, some huge ones, gaping, going downward. Artillery missiles.

We went past the marketplace, bustling with people, and up the hill to the UN Facilities. German guards at the checkpoint looked at our press passes and let us walk to register at the reception. We got our day passes as UN guests and called Mr. Lassen, who came to pick us up.

He took us to the PR head, Philip Arnold, with whom we sat down and talked. I asked him whether there had been any incidents in the reintegration of Vukovar into Croatia.

Hardly any, he said, except now and then we have Croats coming back and shouting obscenities at the people who live in their houses.

No physical fights?

No.

How many Croats have returned so far?

We issued more than fifteen hundred permits to return, but so far only a few more than a hundred have come back.

From what I found out several days later, of a few more than a hundred who had returned to the eastern enclave of Slavonia, only one Croat had by that date returned to Vukovar.

A couple of thousand Serbs had left the town, in fear of what would happen when the Croats came back.

Arnold explained that there were several types of residents in Vukovar. First were the old Serbian population who had stayed throughout. Nobody would bother them; they had the right to stay in their homes. At least half the inhabitants were Serb refugees from Bosnia. They had no place to go because their homes were either destroyed, or Muslims or Croats lived in them. Now these were at risk; Croats coming back who had lost their parents or children in the bombing might be vengeful. That's why the Croats who came into the region needed special permits to drive in; foreigners didn't. In a way, that sounded funny. The area was by the Dayton Accord ceded back to Croatia. The Croat police were supposed to control the customs on the Croatian side of the border with Yugoslavia and all the checkpoints between Eastern Slavonia and the rest of Croatia before the full integration of the area into Croatia. Yet the only people who actually could not travel freely into the area were Croats.

Vukovar is a good showcase for Croatia—the victim city, I said.

For both sides, Arnold said.

How so? It's clear that the Serb forces encircled the town, pounded it, killed civilians.

Jon wanted to meet the forensic team to interview them and take their pictures. Mr. Arnold said that the forensic work was done. The two hundred sixty one Vukovar patients who had been taken out of the hospital and shot by the Serb forces were mostly exhumed, identified, taken to Zagreb, and reburied there.

For the mine work we were too late, according to Arnold. But we could take a ride to sight-see the military installations, of which Arnold, Lassen, and everybody else at the UN seemed proud.

Alexei, a Ukranian pilot, gave us a tour on a UN mini-bus. His English was pretty good, although he spoke slowly and often misunderstood our questions. He had a jovial attitude, blue eyes, and a crew cut; if he hadn't spoken, I would have assumed he was an American soldier.

We stopped and watched the Danube from the western bank of the river, which was fortified against flooding. There were several fishermen and a few flat-bottomed boats. Near the bank was a monument to the wounded soldiers of the Second World War: a woman and a man carrying a wounded soldier, whose shirt was ripped open and brave chest exposed. Now there was an even bigger statement on the monument—a big bullet hole in the chest, as though the wounded soldier had been killed. It was as if even the monuments were being killed, and they of course were: the mass destruction of monuments, churches, and other cultural landmarks was extraordinary. It was impossible to find a church that wasn't demolished, except for a Serb-Orthodox church downtown.

Alexei showed us a grenade that had penetrated the pavement but hadn't exploded. He said we had just missed another sight—three missiles stuck in a large tree. But the tree was cut down and the missiles taken out, for fear they might explode.

Along the way we saw an apartment complex that was shattered, with gaping holes, hanging terraces, blown-out sections. On the ground floor and the second floor people were leaning out the window, watching.

You should see this place at night, said Alexei. It's dark everywhere, except here and there a light, like the asymmetrical eyes of a monster.

Of course, a building like that would be condemned in the States because it could cave in any moment, and there could be mines in it that hadn't exploded.

Jon and I went to the water tower, a huge and precarious concrete structure, thin at the bottom, wide at the top, with serious damage: projectile holes, cement fallen on the ground and strewn all over. A staircase inside looked fairly good. Every fourth step or so was missing, but it kept going up.

Let's go up here, I said to Jon. There must be a good view on top.

He declined, saying it would be sheer lunacy.

I said I had heard of people climbing it, but he said, Just look at it. This thing could crumble at any moment.

From behind an old pizzeria, called Toranj, we saw the Danube again, green even in the sun, perhaps because of the algae and the muddy bottom, the woods on the other side reflected in the water.

The other side of the river was sandy, with poplars curiously all of the same height, as though someone had shaved the tops of the forest. Perhaps the northern winds that sometimes blow from Ukraine do shave off the soft wood treetops. The other bank of the river was in Vojvodina, an autonomous region Serbia had appropriated in 1989; a good deal of shelling of the city took place from the Vojvodina side.

The Franciscan monastery on top of the hill near the pizza restaurant was seriously damaged, or more accurately, destroyed. However, some parts of the fresco were intact, blue like the sky, with Jesus, Mary, and the saints. In other places, sections of the wall were missing from projectile hits. The floor was dusty with many footprints. Clearly one could walk around here. The graffiti were written all over the church, mostly in Cyrillic. One said, *Death to Tudjman*. Another, *Serbs Don't Forgive*. A lot of obscenities.

The Serb church near the center was intact, with a shining copper roof. Near the Hotel Dunav was a small marina with old *chikljas*, flat-bottom boats. The Vuka River, from which came the name of the town, Vukovar, was small and broadened only the last one hundred yards as it descended into the Danube. Sewage pipes led into it.

At the marketplace I ran into the old gate-keeper of the shoe factory, Borovo. It was a famous factory that had employed close to fifty thousand people. Although the factory was largely destroyed, most of it beyond repair, there were more than two thousand workers there now. I asked the guard whether we could tour the factory.

No problem, he said, but first let me ask the factory director.

He returned shortly and said that the director had stepped out. But we could stop by later and no doubt he would give us the permits to come in.

Later on, I ran into him. He recognized me and I him. He was even dressed the same way as when he was at the gate.

What are you doing here? I asked him. Selling cigarettes?

Oh, sure. Got to do something. Can't stay home. I have to moonlight, my salary is too low.

How much do you get paid?

Around a hundred German marks. Not enough to support a family. And how about you? You are a journalist? What newspapers are you working for?

Several of them in the States.

That sounds good. You must make a decent living then.

In the meanwhile, a black market saleswoman came by and said, You work for the Polish television, don't you? I saw you here a week ago. How did the interviews go?

No, I don't work for any TV.

But you are from Poland.

No.

At that she lost interest in talking with me and withdrew. Perhaps she concluded that since I was lying, there was no point conversing with me.

Near the parking lot a dozen men were offering to change money. They were pretty blatant about it. One car almost hit a couple of the money-changers. The traffic was erratic. One-way streets didn't mean one way. So, when we drove around with Alexei and ran into a narrow bridge and a car approaching it, he moved aside and gave the advantage to the other driver, who looked like he was fifteen.

I always give right-of-way to the locals, Alexei said. They drive like crazy.

Let's go to the Rusbat, he suggested.

Rusbat? I asked. Russian battalion?

Yes, that's in UN English, or UNTAES English; we have our own language here. We all say, *Dobar dan* (*good day*), and *Kako ste?* (*how are you?* in Croatian and Serbian), and we have all sorts of expressions that nobody outside the area would understand. Pigeon English, plus some local expressions, plus acronyms, minus grammar.

Near the river we saw a beautiful restaurant, made mostly of oak and glass, jutting into the river, clearly completely new. Jon and I didn't eat anything in Vukovar. Our appetite was spoiled by the sights of destruction, plus gasoline fumes that were leaking in the UN car. The thought of eating in a restaurant that was founded on ashes, perhaps corpses, didn't appeal to us. The blue Danube was the red Danube here.

Which is not to say that many people in Vukovar weren't nice, or victims of war circumstances themselves. When I asked for directions back to Vinkovci, a man was very eager and friendly in explaining how to find the road. Many people are friendly now, perhaps out of fear. They don't know whether they will be able to stay here, whether they will have unpleasant confrontations with the Croats who were evicted, whether they can return to their old homes. It would have been good to talk to several people, but our day was over, and I wasn't in the mood to play journalist and interview people. As soon as something is official, perhaps people will shy away from it. When we asked several people for permission to photograph them, they all declined.

On the way out, I thought there wouldn't be a problem because the border police—a border that had become illegitimate—knew how we'd gotten in. We had gone through several checkpoints in the UN vehicle, and they were all automatic. Just a wave. From up high, the demarcation lines seemed a joke, and we got used to that attitude fast. However, a policeman stopped us here, examined our passports and press credentials, and then asked for the car pass.

You should have registered the car, got the blue pass, he said in Serbian.

Believe me, I tried in Vinkovci, but nobody gives it out there. The one man who does, Mr. Marek, is on vacation.

That's not true, another policeman commented, you can get it there.

You can, but I can't, I said. I gave an account of the rigamarole, and said, Call Mr. Lassen. He called in before so we'd go through. He could easily confirm that.

We don't have his number.

I do. Here it is.

We can't call that number from here.

Why not? It's local, just a kilometer away!

Wait a minute, we need a translator, said the Serb cop. Until then, we'd understood each other perfectly since there isn't much different between Serbian and Croatian. In fact, there wasn't a single word he spoke that I didn't understand, and I was sure he understood every word I said. But now that he again looked at my American passport, he thought it would be easier to talk with me if there were a translator—or, at any rate, he wanted some kind of help. I wanted it, too. A woman translator came who remembered us from before. She said so to the cop, and that it was true, we had permission to enter.

If you take responsibility for them, I will let them through, he said.

I don't have the authority to take any responsibility in such matters; that's not my job, she said.

Where are you registered? the cop asked us.

Why would I be registered?

I mean, where are you staying?

We are traveling.

But you must be staying somewhere.

Hotels wherever we go.

But you must be registered.

Why? The Croatian border police simply let us in. They didn't say we needed a specific location and address reserved in our names before we'd be allowed in.

He was asking old style questions, the kind I used to get at the East German border. Perhaps he didn't know what was expected, and the transitional days, in which several police systems were supposed to cooperate as one, confounded him, so he'd reverted to what he knew best, old style socialism border pestering.

A man from the Fiji Islands, the UN policeman, came along, but his English was hard to understand. He spoke French on the phone. He looked through our press credentials. Called again. Then he said we could go.

I couldn't make any conclusions from having been harassed at the border. Certainly not about nationality. And nothing new about the police. I don't prosper around police. In a way I believe that Police is one nation, bigger than Poland. How many cops are there in the world? Well, their jobs are similar, and they are interchangeable. Not that I need to generalize about them either...

Worrying about the police made us forget temporarily the impressions of the day. If it's so easy for visitors to forget after a bit of discomfort, who will remember Vukovar? Nearly eight thousand people died in Vukovar and the vicinity, and close to three thousand in a couple of days in November when Serb forces went through the city, house to house, dragging people out of cellars and sewage pipes, shooting them in the streets and cornfields.

Of course, Serbs don't forget, as the graffito goes, the atrocities that the Croatian *ustashas* committed against them in World War II. That was repeated in school over and over by history teachers when I was a pupil in Croatia. Many Croats don't forget the slaughters that the Serb nationalist *chetniks* committed on the Croatian rural population, although that lesson was passed over in silence in our history lessons. My brother-in-law—who died of stomach cancer, and who had spent the recent war two hundred yards away from the Serb border toward Vukovar, from where his street was shelled almost daily—told me that when he was a child, during World War II, he ran into a ditch full of Croatian peasants massacred by *chetniks*. He never forgot, and wasn't even allowed to talk about it because he would be jailed for spreading nationalist propaganda. He told me this in the park after my father's funeral, at a moment when we were both talking about life, death, and souls. Which is better, to forget or to remember? Of course, to remember, but not to abuse the memories as Serbian leaders have done to spur their armies into aggression against Croats and Muslims.

Croats will remember Vukovar. Muslims will remember Srebrenica. And what is the lesson? Not to trust thy neighbor? But that's perhaps where the trouble began and will resume.

TWO CROATIAS

MY BEING FROM CROATIA has been a source of much painful misunderstanding. During the recent war, many people felt sorry for me, and others were ready to treat me as a mass murderer. And now, a decade later, they treat me as a tourist guide.

In 1991, when the war in Croatia started, my sister was gravely wounded by shrapnel in Vinkovci and operated on without electricity. Vukovar fell with three thousand people slaughtered by Serbian and Yugoslav forces in a couple of days. Yet in the American press there was little sympathy for Croatia, and a lot of simplified history vilifying Croatia. I had many conversations where I was on the defensive, and this is what I remember from one of them, during a Thanksgiving dinner, where a literary critic asked me, When did you escape from Croatia?

I haven't escaped from anywhere. I've lived in the States for twenty years and haven't escaped yet.

Are your relatives still there?

Still? They don't plan to come here. Do you think everybody wants to come here?

Can you explain the war to me and all that ethnic hatred? This has been going on for centuries.

It hasn't. Just now and then there is a war, but usually it's imported from abroad—bigger countries fighting for the terrain. We oscillate, a few years of war, then twenty-thirty of peace. We forget fast and then we suddenly remember. This is our first original, un-imported war. Actually, Milosevic and his generals exported the war to Croatia to create Greater Serbia.

But wasn't Croatia helping the Germans in World War Two, and you killed hundreds of thousands of Serbs?

I didn't kill anybody. True, the puppet regime in Croatia committed a lot of atrocities. On the other hand, Tito, who led the liberation war against the Germans, was a Croat, as were many of his partisans. It was a civil war, fought in a defeated country, Yugoslavia, whose Serbian king had signed a pact with Hitler.

Croatians as Catholics, didn't they collaborate with Mussolini? And Tudjman, isn't he a fascist?

Who isn't? He was Tito's youngest general and he contributed to defeating the Germans more than any current head of state in Europe who enjoys labeling him. But I thought we were talking about the current war, not the old wars! What about protecting Croatia and Bosnia now? Bad historical analysis won't accomplish that!

My academic friend regarded me with what appeared to me a mix of cynicism, pity, and suspicion. He probably didn't mean it that way, but I was irritated enough to feel hounded.

I got used to treating Croatia as some kind of burden—so when people asked me about where to travel in the Balkans, I usually advised them to go to Slovenia and Greece. And then, suddenly, Croatia became tourist destination number one for the Lonely Planet and many tourist journals. Nevertheless, I wasn't ready for the conversation I had a few days ago in Murmansk, Russia. A professor of linguistics asked me, You left Croatia for the United States? How could you do that?

What do you mean, how could I? America was the place to be.

I just came back from Croatia, and it's the most beautiful country in the world.

I wouldn't go that far. What about all those sharp rocks and sea urchins that end up in your feet if you take a step away from the beach?

All those islands, and the old towns, which look like Italy, but are better because they haven't been ruined by commercialism. It's heaven on earth! The cheap country wine, the figs! The men and women are so tall. . .

Sure, they spend too much time in the sun and eat sardines with small bones in them.

And you have all those tennis players and skiers.

Yes, there's not much economy so people excel at hobbies.

The people were really friendly.

All the unfriendly, hateful, and aggressive ones got killed in the war.

You are joking? If I were you, I'd be very proud to come from there, I'd go right back. America is a desert compared with Croatia.

I am not going back.

She looked at me as if I was a madman. I was struck—first my relatives seemed to be crazy for not leaving Croatia, and now I am crazy for not living in Croatia.

I was sunk in gloom for the rest of the day, thinking maybe I had spent most of my life in the wrong place.

What difference a mere ten years make! I wish people had a bit more memory, so they wouldn't present a mono-dimensional picture of the country. During the war, it wasn't all horror: those islands were still there, and weren't much affected by the war. And now, there's still complicated history with unresolved ethnic problems. I am always a bit out of step. I praised the country when it was under attack, and now that it's praised, I am such a pessimist that a critic in the Croatian press said that I seem to remember only the worst things about Croatia, which in my stories turns out to be a gloomy, drunken, and murderous country. True, I am tired of all the tourist praise the country gets now as I was tired of all the venom it got before. It is a complex country deserving of no reductionism.

BERLIN JOURNAL

Summer 2002

THE FLIGHT FROM FRANKFURT to Berlin was delayed because of
me. The announcement on the plane, in German, was: We are
missing one passenger whose baggage is on the plane. It will
take some ten minutes to examine the bags and we will be on
our way. A security man in yellow passed by my seat and called
my name. The ticket slip that would have registered me wasn't
passed through the machine when I got on. By the time the
announcer was ready to repeat the announcement in English,
the guards discovered me on the plane. I hadn't discovered
myself yet, but they did.

In Berlin, Tegel Airport, I got a taxi. A sad-looking Iranian
man with a thick and drooping mustache, better than Stalin's,
drove me to the first address, where my friend Joyce would
meet me and give me my orientation about teaching a writing
course at the Freie Universität in Berlin. The man said he was
from Persia. He claimed the Shah had been wonderful, and
that Iran would not recover during his lifetime. He had not
been home in twenty-five years and didn't plan to go. The

weather was cool, so I said, Wonderful weather in the summer, isn't it?

Horrible, he replied.

We drove along a river with small bridges over which bikers rode. Berlin looked green and calm, and I enjoyed the sensation. I remembered how James Joyce said, Dublin was a new sensation. Berlin was a new sensation to me now. No matter that I had been here twenty years ago. I had been mostly in East Berlin, for a month. This to me seemed like an entirely different city, as though I had landed in Amsterdam, and was somewhere away from the center along a canal.

I visited first my writer friend from NY, Joyce Hackett, and her friend, Morrison, a Scottish woman who translates from the German and lives in the second Hinterhof near Suedstern subway stop. You go from one yard into another, and in the back is her apartment. Berlin used to be arranged so that the most prosperous families lived in the front, those a little less prosperous around the first yard, and so on. Some apartment complexes are complex indeed, containing up to eight yards. The last one used to be for the poorest ones, and for lower tradesmen, such as cobblers and smiths. From Morrison's window, you could see a cemetery across the wall. "My neighbor sometimes stops by to take a look at her dead husband's and son's resting place. She likes to see it from as many angles as possible. Of course, that gives her a chance to talk about them interminably."

For a meal, Joyce and I went outside, two doors down from the gate to the street. We had *Zanderfisch* special, for nine euro a piece. The price was also marked in DMs as Germans were still getting used to the euro. The meal was done medium rare, on a bed of tomatoes, garlic, and eggplant.

Next table to our heavy wooden one sat two young men gazing into each other's eyes, sipping red wine, and occasionally kissing on the lips. And when they were not doing that, they were visibly following our conversation; Joyce tended to speak pretty voluminously, and she spoke so fast that she would run out of breath. She talked about what she liked her students to see in Berlin, how to observe, and how the beginning writers seemed to see so little that she liked to have them all observe the same thing, write about it, and read what they had written to one another, so they could see what other people saw. "If you put all of their observations together, you have just enough for a good essay." I don't know what the two young men thought of that. Maybe if I'd had their observations as well, I would make a good scene out of the restaurant meal, but OK, I haven't, and I will leave it in. It's a journal, so let it be whatever it's going to be. Isn't that the relaxing advantage of writing a journal, that you don't have to judge it, whether it is good enough? The scene is not vivid enough, but so what? It's not a damned story. Many journals are written and never read again—I have kept journals which I never read again, and dutifully lost them. Aren't journals something that children and grandchildren read to find out what their ancestors were like? I doubt that my grandchildren if I ever get them will read the above scene—and should I pepper it, in case they do? No, let it stay as is, unpeppered, German-food bland.

After that, I took another cab ride, to my address at 2 Ringslebenstrasse, to apartment #99. My driver turned out to be another Persian. He first took out his map, put on his glasses, and said, this way it will be cheaper for you because I will find out the most direct route. He too had loved the Shah, but unlike the first driver, he was willing to cooperate with the new Iranian government. That's the only chance, he said. Liberal ideas from outside will help the change. My staying out will not accomplish anything. I am a geologist—I will get my doctorate in two weeks—and they can use my knowledge. And I love the terrain there—it is so rich geologically. Germany isn't. There's hardly anything here except coal.

It was late in the evening, nearly eleven, and pretty dark near my temporary apartment. Near the main entrance, wrote Jens, the director of the summer program, in an email, you will find a small staircase to your left going down one flight of stairs. On the wall, you will see a set of safe boxes, and next to them, a numeric keyboard. Type in 1836, and one of the safe doors will pop open. In the safe is your key for room #99.

True, just as he wrote, so it was. No need for personal contact, for picking up at the airport, and so on, the way things are done elsewhere. Here, technology can take care of it. When I entered the apartment complex, I saw nobody. I took the elevator to the second floor, and went through the mazes of corridors until I found number 99. Small apartment with one bedroom and a shower, no bath, and a well-equipped kitchen, with a corkscrew and a bottle opener.

When I accumulated garbage three days later, I wondered where to take it. I found a garbage courtyard, fenced in and locked. That certainly made sure no human scavenger would come in and rummage through garbage. In St. Petersburg, in Russia, there are usually two-three bums at the same time digging through large iron tanks full of garbage in the middle of the courtyards, even in the center of the city. They take bottles, which they can turn in for a ruble a bottle, plastic sacs, and all sorts of things, even a bite to eat. Some desperate drunks tilt the bottles they find. So, there is no need of recycling bins there—the poor recycle everything. When I had accumulated some fifty glass bottles in St. Petersburg, I brought them out as a present to the bums, and they celebrated their luck—I could see their spirits lifted; one bum took one bag of bottles, another another, and off they went with their catch.

I walk in the streets. I look for the Wall. It is not there, of course, but not even the traces are. I remember, in former East Berlin, how startling it was to see the wall cut some streets. The street would go straight into the wall. It would continue on the other side, in another world. At least one street should have remained like that, walled, to remind people of the old division.

I talked to Jens, who comes from Berlin, and he says he can't remember exactly where the wall stood. He says many people complain about that, that they don't remember any more. The wall came down. . .

Today in the passage near Alexanderplatz, from the TV tower to the Passaustrasse, I saw a young woman playing balalaika, the Lara song from *Doctor Zhivago.* She lifted her gaze to meet mine. One side of her face smiled, the other didn't. I don't know whether it was her east side or her south side which smiled, but the smile looked like disenchantment. Her hair was curly, I couldn't tell the color of her eyes from the distance, they weren't fully open anyway, and her face was round, broad. She was probably Russian. I wondered how this music sounded to many former East Germans, who had hated Russia and perhaps still do. It was a strange form of sentimental incursion, not exactly colonialism, but nomadism. She smiled again when I saw her several hours later, with one half of her face, and played some other sentimental melody, which I wasn't familiar with. I did not give her money. I didn't talk with her. Some encounters without a word spoken linger with me more than encounters with conversations.

I ate a grilled chicken half under the S-Bahn of Alexanderplatz. Another man did likewise. A woman ate a huge frankfurter, a thick one, and her daughter laughed, and as she dipped the sausage into the yellow sauce, the passersby laughed. Three African guys bought a chicken and trivided it. A cold blue wind blew—strange for the end of July.

Several days later, I looked at the paragraph above and it occurred to me that I would not remember the chicken and frankfurters if I had not written it all down. Well, I would remember it, but it would not readily pop up in my head, and so it appears to me that journals are worth writing to collect the details. Sure, collecting details is like collecting small change. . . years have to pass before they gain in value. First they lose in value with the general inflation, but then they gain as the era which they represented slips away, and the coins can retrieve memories. . . I already see old East German five-mark coins sold for twenty euro, while they used to be worth only one in 1983 when I was there. On Oranienburgstrasse, a block away from the Synagogue that was burnt down by the Nazis and afterward further damaged by the Allied bombing, there is a large numismatic store, and the DDR coins here have reached surprising levels. Well, in principle what I am saying is right, but it's hard for me to see how even in a hundred years, people eating thick frankfurters would be an amazing thing, but who knows, maybe it will be—maybe people will be so enlightened eventually that they won't eat crap like that. Anyway, I am not writing this for posterity or posteriority. This is a journal, meandering along with me in Berlin, and I am not sure I will ever read it myself unless writing counts as reading. I think I write a journal to think in the moment, or to pretend to think, or at least to try to think, but maybe the journal is keeping me away from the experience the way taking photographs tends to keep people away from the sites they are picturing.

I took a walk from Friedrichstrasse Station. That appears to be the train station from which I left in 1983 and in 1988. Then, it was a threatening place, with policemen carrying machine guns and parading around with dogs. Today I walked out to a commercial paradise of stores and of—policemen with machine guns and German shepherds. In fact, there were more police now than then. As I walked up from the train station, up Friedrichstrasse to Oranienburger Tor, I passed by dozens of police vans. The police lined the streets. Many of them smoked, some played cards, one of them joked with a passenger, and not far from them, on a wall, sat a bunch of grimy Eurotrash, with a hairstyle I wasn't sure was dreadlocks or simply unwashed hair that got entangled, dirty clothes, tattoos, chains, piercings all over, dirty nails, bloodshot eyes. They begged for change. Berlin is a large city, but still, I ran into two women I had seen on the U-bahn. They had talked about how to lose weight. One was telling another that she ought to eat nothing but protein— meats, tofu, eggs—and salads. And for it to work, she needed to have a nutrition guru. They were equally overweight, and this was clearly theoretical rather than practical knowledge. They sat at a sidewalk café where people ate nicely. In fact, most of the street, Oranienburg, was nice. People walked up and down. Yellow trams stopped. It was like the Village in NYC in a way, and in a way not. Up the street I saw more police behind a fence, near the synagogue and the Jewish museum. Clearly, the government was afraid of what skinheads and neo-Nazis could do—the government wanted no embarrassment on that score. That seemed a strange way to respect a religion but these days, with such a large Arab population in Berlin, after 9/11—the attacks could come not only from neo-Nazis but also from the PLO and other enemies of Israel. The police stood alert, scrutinizing the crowds passing by. That attitude I had seen in the police guarding the American embassy in Sarajevo, except there it was more aggressive, machine guns at the ready, and the policemen eyeing every car, peering into it. The Synagogue was built in the Moor style, and from a distance I couldn't tell whether it would be a mosque or a synagogue. The roof is gilded, and during the sunset, from the other side of the street, it reflected light magnificently. In the background, the clouds were dark, and the hole in the clouds from which the light shone was an exception. The light soon disappeared, and it grew dark quickly. In front of the Synagogue, I almost collided with a young dandy with long hair who wore a short tee-shirt to show off his abdominal muscles and the hair beneath his navel.

A block away, girls lined the streets on the sidewalks and stood in the road off the curb. I didn't see anybody stop by to pick them up, nor did any pedestrians come over to talk to them. I did not know what the laws were, but clearly, with so many police around, prostitution could be curbed unless it was legal. I wondered how many of them came from Moldavia and other poor ex-Soviet republics. Most prostitutes wore something tacky. It wasn't even the amount of flesh revealed—some of the women sitting crosslegged in the sidewalk cafes revealed more—but the style; the extra-high heels, the fur collar atop an extra-short leather jacket. . . Even there, just a block before the Synagogue, a young woman taking a picture of her friends showed more of her abdomen in low jeans. You could see her hip bones. It seems each era fetishizes one part of the female body. For a while it was thighs, clavicles, the breast bone, but now it's the hip bones. If you can show your hipbones, you needn't show anything else—the lean belly and the hipbone make a statement of being in good shape, or being brave. At any rate, it was the tacky style, the gaudy colors, the strong makeup, that made the statement of commerce. To me it made sense—commerce to me always appears tacky, no matter how fancied up the stores may be.

Back to the bones. Jaw bones are always in fashion. Any proof, in fact, that you aren't fat is in fashion. She has beautiful bones. I heard that expression for the first time when I got to the States. I hadn't heard anything like it in Croatia, where, when I was a kid, flesh was adored. If you were fat, you were called *Jak*, which didn't mean the bovine animal but strong. Women's thighs were admired; the hourglass figure was too. That all has changed even in the Mediterranean, but still, perhaps because it's easier to be thin there, there is still no such emphasis on the bones. This calcification of beauty may be morbid. Of course, it's a reaction to the general fattening of the world. When fatness was an exception, it was part of the canon of beauty. Now that leanness is an exception, its symptoms are canonized. Beautiful bones. But right next to the synagogue, that had a strange and alarming ring to me, the whole notion of calcification of the beauty canon, the boning up of the ideal beauty.

When I took the U-Bahn at the end of my walk, one stop north of Alexanderplatz, line #8, I saw the same bony peacock man with pubic hair above his low-cut jeans. He was talking to a blond ten-year old boy, asking him, Do you like pretty women? A woman sitting on the other side of the bench, who was pretty, laughed at that. We all ended up in the same wagon, and now the man was talking nonsense to another man, who just shook his head inimically.

The young woman stroked her lower lip with her forefinger for a long time. To me it seemed a peculiar motion, perhaps erotic, perhaps thoughtful. Now, erotic to whom? To her? Maybe; maybe she stimulated and pleased her senses that way. To the spectators? Maybe. It looked gentle and attractive, caught attention and captivated it. Later I saw another pretty woman with long hair lift her head, looking toward the TV screen where commercials show up so the subway ride won't totally be wasted for capitalism—she took a chapstick and kept massaging her lips with it, slowly. A man on a bike (many people in Berlin take their bicycles into the subway trains), who was drinking from a can of beer, said, looking at the woman's face, *Das tut Weh*! That hurts. He looked around then to see whether anybody heard him, and he made eye contact with me, and kept nodding his head. OK, so I wasn't the only one noticing this. Sometimes I think, Look what's going on. I almost congratulate myself thinking I am the only one, but no, this seems to be the "human condition" that fellow sojourners on public transportation go through: they observe and pretend that they don't. That level of covert observation, well, what can I say, I like that for a change. It is much more entertaining and provocative than what you experience driving a car long distance, which I did quite a few times in Nebraska and Pennsylvania, and as a rule, I had old cars that didn't have radios, so driving was a test of imagination. This sensory deprivation tank carried me across the uniform landscapes, where, true, I appreciated every cottonwood in Nebraska, and every river and ridge in Pennsylvania, but nevertheless got dreadfully bored, unlike in the U-Bahn, where boredom for now seemed impossible to me as I scrutinized passengers.

I got out at Gopius Passage, where a new mall covers several acres of land, or rather, asphalt. Going up the stairs, I realized just how aging Germany was. There were a few dozen grayhaired and bluehaired people walking up the stairs slowly. A couple of women gripped the railing on the side of the stairs, going up. Several men limped, with their sticks pushed against the stairs. An obese aging woman gasped midway up the stairs and caught her breath. I couldn't find a way to go past the people. Of course, in twenty or ten years, who knows, I might be walking up the stairs at this pace, gasping. I wondered, were they a group? I hadn't seen them in the subway. Where did they come from?

I am teaching a course on travel writing at the Freie Universität. That is why I indulge myself by keeping a travel journal. I don't think I would have started otherwise, but now that I am in it, I am enjoying it. Well, at least in this room. Instead of an office, I have a small classroom. Jens, the director, promised I would have a computer hookup, but I don't. All the better for it—I am not tempted to "surf." I think that even at home, in my studio,

I will not have internet. I should not have a phone either. This is good, being in an ugly classroom. The walls are all white, the door is bright yellow, the floor is carpeted green, and the tables are plastic white. The windows are huge, they cover a whole wall, or rather, uncover it. I see the aluminum structure of the next line of offices and classrooms. The university main building is constructed as a series of corridors with offices; and each corridor is named a Strasse. I am off the main street, K, in KJ 26 #129, in other words between the aluminum corridor/tubes J and K. Getting around here is like getting around Manhattan and certain sections of Minneapolis—a rational system. Americans built this university as a present to West Berlin, because Humboldt Universität had been taken over by the Soviets, and was mainly behind the wall. Of course, in fact the Freie, the free university, was surrounded by walls, and this cage was supposed to represent freedom, while whatever was outside it was slavery under communism. That is how most people on both sides of the wall in the end understood it—that the small circle, West Berlin, was the free part. At any rate, when you look at the old map, it's hard to imagine that that is how it should be. So, this university is an American project, and it has a bit of a slummy feel to it on the main campus. But outside, in Dahlem-Lam, one of the most expensive neighborhoods of Berlin, it's a large park with mansions and elegant buildings. Some of them are various departments of the university. The Plank Physics Institute is here. Anyway, my classroom. When I got in, the curtains were down. Suddenly, they began to lift with a buzz. I wondered whether I had triggered them by passing by a sensor, but as I looked out, I noticed that the curtains were being lifted on all the offices at the same time. They are outside the windows, thus really keeping the sunlight heat outside, if necessary, and also protecting the glass in storms. I looked at my watch. It was precisely eleven am. I wondered whether every morning at eleven am all the window shades go up. No privacy now—I can peep into many offices. Well, that is what it should be like; public universities are public. Some offices have inside curtains, and a couple of the curtains were being drawn now. Maybe when there is enough light outside, the curtains go up, with some light sensor. I don't know, and I won't find out. I could find out, but I don't think I will get around to that, to asking. Maybe I could read about it. Now I notice that there is a little button that you can turn to "Auf" and "Zu"—open and close. I tried *zu*. Great, the curtains are going down. Maybe the university has a certain program that makes the curtains go up through central control, but you can get them to go down. I have written a wonderfully boring paragraph above—a very German one, at least I imagine it that way. *All too German.*

In the dining hall, there are options for different kinds of meals. One of them is bio, or organic. I went to that line yesterday and got a mound of burnt potatoes with cream. The cream was the protein part, I guess. The food is not great but, therefore, the beer is. Many students get a pint of beer with their meals. *Bier ist Nahrung.* Food. I wonder how much knowledge the students retain after one of these lunches. They are subsidized, the lunches are, and even the beer is included. What a contrast to the "dry" campuses of America! On many campuses, even formal receptions can't take place with wine— that sinful liquid has to be consumed outside, somewhere. Strange pilgrim's progress, from holy communion with wine, to those dry receptions.

I should write something deeper about Berlin and its history but I don't bother. A lot of deep writing has been done about it. A lot of deep writing has been done about Russia, and I have seen a lot of bad writing about the cemeteries there, the siege of Leningrad, which originated from this "twin" city. I could go to the cemeteries here, to the bunkers, to the variety of *Gedächtnis* monuments, to reflect on the terrors of World War Two, but the world war is much beyond me. There's hardly any evidence of the Wall anymore. There is evidence of the war, artificially kept up (they could have repaired that torn church by now), even though the city has changed. Today I saw Prime Minister Sharon interviewed on TV, following Israel's bombing of an apartment complex in Gaza, which killed fifteen people, mostly kids. I saw a gruesome picture of paramedics trying to revive a baby. Anyway, Sharon said that Germany is one of Israel's best friends. Namely, Germany is capable of so much change. I read a history book, I forget where, written in the 19th century, in which one sentence startled me. It went something like this, Traditionally, the greatest German problem has been the lack of military organization. That changed, didn't it? After 1870, people didn't keep reflecting on the lack of military organization. Yes, it's good to reflect on the dangers of Germany, but I don't know what I can contribute to that other than my scant knowledge and prejudice. To walk around and see a murderer in every person I see in the street. . . well, I could do that, it would fit my misanthropic mood. I am not interested, however, in doing global history here, or, for that matter, world politics. Quite a few people are here to study the European Union. Perhaps there is such a thing as the European Union. When I am on the bus, I don't see or feel any union. I see all sorts of things, but that sort of big newspaper-headlines knowledge is not with me, nor do I want it to shape the phenomenology of the place. What do I see, hear, here and now, what is my *Dasein* in Berlin. But clearly, I am doing a poor job of it, of staying away from history, for even as I excuse myself for not covering the big topics, I keep mentioning them. Yes, history is large here, it looms; many buildings are dark, and not only visually. At the same time, my tourist guidebook states flatly that Berlin has little history to show. Most buildings were built after World War II, since more bombs were dropped into the eight hundred square kilometers here than on all of Great Britain in the war. Most of this area was devastated. Even many of the old-looking buildings are simply fakes, replicas, pretending to be the original history. I saw the Brandenburg Gate the other day, or rather, pretended to see it. It was all covered in large blue and brown boards. Clear sky was painted between painted columns. In other words, you could only see the painting of Brandenburg Gate, which was being repaired and restored behind the stage-set. Of course, the set itself is prettier than the real thing behind—it has blue sky, while the real thing would show only gray sky and big clouds. In a way it doesn't matter which Brandenburg Gate I am seeing, and whether the dome of Der Dom, the cathedral on the Museum Island, is the original one or not. All the same to me. It's all a showy stage now. Checkpoint Charlie is now a museum. There is much less than meets the eye, as the saying goes. And of course, there is much more.

There are immigrants from all over the world here. I see Turkish signs, with their umlauts, and Albanian, and Kurdish. My bus passed by Dalmacija restaurant. So, there are Croats here. Of course there are. I am not meeting them; I am not eager to see them. I should be, because I may write about them, but it won't be the same Croats. It will be some people out of my imagination, whom I will call Croatian for the hell of it, but they will not accurately correspond to Croats, nor do I think that accurate correspondence is possible, not even in journalism. For that reason, perhaps I should not use such names.

Wannsee. I took an S-Bahn there. This is where Heinrich von Kleist killed himself. I wanted to look for the exact spot where he drank ten bottles of wine with his girlfriend before killing her and himself according to a *Bund* that they made. A couple of old men played accordion music, some German folk music. Passersby laughed at it. Boats, docked in the harbor, offered rides over seven lakes and back. I took the train two stations back, to another lake, which seemed to be the most popular—people lay everywhere on the grass. Many people walked along the waterfront, some rode bikes, others walked their dogs. One dog swam. You could rent boats and row. Anyway, the beach atmosphere pretty soon made it clear to me why I was not at the Adriatic—I find the sun-struck atmosphere tedious. Sunday. On the way back, I bought coffee at Einstein Kaffee on Ku'damm. Good coffee is hard to come by, even in this metropolis; EK makes the best coffee. An old man stood behind me in the line and smiled, revealing large teeth. I said, *Er macht es gut. Ja*, he agreed, *ganz artistisch.* The old man later sat outside and drank his coffee with a great deal of visible pleasure, sighing. Then he stood up and walked, perhaps home. In the train, I read a special issue of *Der Spiegel,* about the Germans who had been driven out in ethnic cleansing campaigns at the end of World War One. Almost three million from Sudetenland. The Czechs, who offered hardly any resistance to the Germans, celebrated the victory given them by Russians in such a manner. Poland, Yugoslavia, Germans were driven out of these countries, mass executed. The story is not given much attention because people are put in the mass category—Germans, the perpetrators, not the victims. Well, are they all the same? Did they all vote the same way? Those in other countries didn't vote at all, and their sympathies may have been largely with the invading armies, but it is not these Germans who decided anything or started anything. If the US were suddenly to lose a war that Bush initiates, should all the Americans be driven out from everywhere, be mass executed, all on account of being Americans, even if Bush didn't win the presidency with a majority vote? Hitler, likewise, never got the majority, but worked with coalitions. If one is not to romanticize, and permanently divide nations into the good ones and the bad ones, and thus perpetrate chauvinism, all these stories have to be told.

I watched a two-hour documentary on the rebuilding of the Dresden *Frauenkirche*. I remember visiting the site in 1983. It was merely a rubble of rocks. I climbed a few rocks with a drunk East German who had waited for the same train as I. Whole sections of the city were still left in rubble, and it appeared in the center to be largely a ghost town. In West Berlin, just one church was left destroyed, but still standing, as a monument, and even so, the lines where the steeple fell off were solidly cut and copper was placed over them to prevent further erosion.

No such luck in Dresden until the Iron Curtain melted. A Nobel Prize winner in medicine who had been thrown out of Silesia as a boy at the end of the war remembered Dresden, and how horrifying it looked all destroyed. He gave nearly his entire award to the foundation for rebuilding the Dresden cathedral. Each rock was identified from pictures before the war, in terms of shading, shape, and so on, and restored, and then placed into the walls of the cathedral, so that one could say it was made out of the same stone. Bach had praised the cathedral for its wonderful acoustics. And now the cathedral is restored enough for concerts to take place in it. The destruction of Dresden was an overkill. It was done in February, 1945, when it was clear that Germany would lose the war. Russians could have already swept across the country but they waited for some reason. Firebombing mostly old people and children and women, hardly any of them culprits in the war, wasn't the most ethical thing to do, but it was done, and now, watching the restoration of the cathedral, which takes place for years and takes millions of dollars, it is clear how much easier destruction is than construction. Much of Berlin is being reconstructed as well, but too much of it simply in the modern style.

Outside the walls of Reichstag, at the beginning of the Tiergarten Park, there was a sign saying in this spot was such and such shot in 1963, trying to cross into West Berlin. OK, a one-sentence paragraph out of the blue, but a good reminder of the past.

I sat at a Seagfredo coffee shop under the elevated Schnellzug station at Berlin Alexanderplatz staring at the TV tower. The mist had just lifted and I could see the ball where the restaurant, two hundred fifteen meters above the ground, was supposed to turn twice a day, giving you a great view. I didn't think I would go up because the visibility was not great, but then it occurred to me that it might be nice to be up in the mist, with hardly any visitors around. So I went up. The restaurant was closed, but the observation deck worked. Actually, most of the famous sights of Berlin were visible, though I couldn't see far. Inner Berlin is not that large, not even with both sides of the city reunited. On the other hand, most of the sights were in the former East Berlin. The Brandenburg Gate, which I could see, used to be the Western Gate of the city, and the old sites were near Alexanderplatz. It seemed strange that Alexanderplatz was named after the Russian tzar, probably because of family ties to the German monarchy. At any rate, being up there, I used the paradigm of being on another tall building, the twin towers of the World Trade Center in New York City, where I had gone to the top four times. Maybe it's cheesy to make such comparisons, but anyway, I did—as I looked out, through the tinted glass. There were no other tall buildings to look at; I had to look down, and there I didn't run into geometry, such as would be easy on the flat terrain, but winding and curving streets, many red roofs, and yards, the Spree River, ruins here and there, and lots of churches, a synagogue with a golden roof.

From high up, it was interesting to read a couple of sentences from *Berlin Alexanderplatz* by Doeblin, which are supposed to give you the spirit of the place. Under each window is one letter marked in the aluminum wall. The rotating restaurant, which turns quickly, seemed to make some people nauseated. Giovanna from Italy complained about it. Ben, a half-German, half-English guy, pointed out that the Reichstag was built outside the original wall since the Kaiser did not like the idea of a parliament, naturally. It was paid for with the war reparations by France.

Was tempted to take a cab to the airport but because I had spent more money than I had planned, I decided to take the train, U-Bahn, to the Tegel Express bus. My U-Bahn made twenty-five stops and took about an hour before getting to the airport bus. It occurred to me that I had not written a single letter during my entire stay in Berlin, and I was leaving after these five weeks. In my head, for the hell of it, I pretended that I was writing a letter to my favorite German writer, and here's an approximation of what I imagined I would write to him.

Letter to Heinrich von Kleist

Guten Morgen, Heinrich!

That is, if there are mornings in the afterlife. Now for several years I wanted to write to you to tell you something that has been bothering me. Namely, why the hell does even your death sound like a story? It's so amazingly well staged in a beautiful setting, at Wannsee, under a willow tree, that it's hard for me to believe that you didn't write the account. I visited the place where now people sail and sun-starved northern German girls sunbathe topless, and I wonder how many of them think of you and your suicide pact with your ill girlfriend. Were you only helping her and making sure she did not feel alone as she exited this life in your violent kind of euthanasia? Or were you sick of life and you wanted to exit it in good company? But let me tell you one thing: all the stories you wrote, each one of them, is better than the script of your suicide. It's too bad that your worst story cost you your life. I think you are the best short story plotter ever, so I am not surprised that even your death was plotted by you. So you drank thirty cups of coffee before dissing yourself? Well, those days, from what I read, the coffee was pretty watery, and if it tasted anything like diner coffee in the States, I think suicide would be better than thirty cups of it. And then you drank ten bottles of red wine? Now that is a little excessive. That is how much Alexander the Great drank, and that was enough to finish him off. And he drank strong southern wine. I imagine you drank some awful German red wine. I've never had luck with German reds from the north. I imagine drinking weak red wine would be depressing too. Plus, didn't the waiters try to cheat you and mix the wine with water? Anyway, sometimes I feel guilty when I write a poor story. I should feel guilty more often, but to die for conceiving a mediocre short story, my friend? I do think you went freaking too far. God, and just to think of it, after you left, Goethe was alone as the king and he could not write one single good story—lots of fine hot air and poetry, but not a single story that would be even as good as your suicide. I keep re-reading your stories and they keep getting better and better for me. Pardon the old wine cliché. Still, I want to ask you, how much of your suicide is real? And how much of it is fiction? No matter what, I miss you, *mein Freund.* But not enough to want to join you, for at least another fifty years.

Josip

WHY I CAN'T WRITE EROTICA

In New York, my word-processing coworker at a law firm wrote erotic novellas on the side, for a thousand dollars each, and it took her two weeks to write one. She claimed that she could not write anything else—she'd tried. I thought it had to be the easiest kind of writing, especially since I had erotic daydreams, but I had other, less compromising, things to write about. Once I ran out of things to say, I would write a terrific erotic story.

Well, one evening, ten years later, I sat in front of my amber screen and couldn't think of a thing to say. The phone rang. Hello, this is Lily Pond, editor of *Yellow Silk* Magazine. I've liked your piece in *Manoa* Magazine. I think you could write a terrific erotic story, couldn't you?

Sure, why not?

It would be for a Doubleday anthology, international erotica, and the pay would be about a thousand dollars.

I had a draft of an erotic story from several years before. In several cases, rewriting an old draft proved to be the best way of writing stores for me—coupling my old and my new ways of writing, sifting for the advantages of both. It worried me that by now the sexual situation in the story seemed hackneyed—a threesome, two men, one woman. But the setting, Lyons,

France, and the protagonists, a punk couple and a Polish solidarity exile, should make it entertaining and fresh enough. My characters seemed to me drawn roundly enough, the erotic descriptions weren't crass, blow by blow, offensive, or violent, and I refined them as much as I could in two days. Eagerly, I mailed the piece off.

Four days later, Lily Pond left a message with my wife, to call.

Whenever an editor calls, it's an acceptance, unless it's the *New York Times* Magazine, whose editors, whenever they turn down a piece, call you up to let you know. They do it out of courtesy, so you'd know you were free to mail the piece elsewhere before it ceased to be timely. The timeliness factor could not play a role here. What was erotic once might be erotic forever, or at least for a century.

I called Lily Pond right back.

I think you could do better, Lily Pond said. This piece just doesn't work for me. I know, it has many fine descriptions of the landscape, characters, funny dialogue, but your erotic scenes aren't effective.

Are they too graphic, or. . . ?

No, they just aren't exciting. I did not get sexually excited reading them. That's the ultimate criterion.

Should I describe more?

I don't know what you should do, but read them out loud, and you'll see what I mean. Read them to your lover.

I'm married, I don't have a lover.

Hum, that's too bad. Your wife could be your lover. Read it to her and see if she gets aroused.

I'm sure she might get aroused, but not erotically—she might get angry that I wrote that.

And another thing—the story gets too complex, politically, psychologically, and too depressing. When you write another story, we have enough time yet, don't worry about being deep and serious—just write several good honest fucking scenes, all right?

O.K. I'll see whether I can do it.

Why couldn't you?

Well, if you'd undergone a decade of feminist censorship, you'd probably write nothing erotic either.

I was surprised that I had come up with that excuse, but censorship, external or internal, did affect me. I began to write while I studied theology at Yale, and I showed my writings to people in the English literature department as well as to preachers. I had the notion that if I was fond of a woman, I could court her by showing her my writings. Many people, however, approached literature as authors' symptoms, and one disease that women often looked for was male chauvinism. One Englishwoman asked me how many stories I'd written, and I said, Ten.

How many from a female POV?

None.

Good-bye.

Now that upset me. If a woman wrote only from a female POV, as M. Duras did, well, that was praiseworthy. Still, although I wrote at the time fairly autobiographically, I agreed that I should be able to write from a female POV, and I did. So on one occasion, where a woman seemed to be fond of me and there was not much need of impressing—she even dedicated poems to me—I gave her a story in which a woman cooks so well that all her husbands die. Next time I rang the bell at her apartment, she would not open the door. She said, I don't know whether I can trust you anymore. Eventually she did open the door, but there was a distance between us now, because my writing was obviously sexist. I said, All right, I come from Yugoslavia, where chauvinism is a way of life. Maybe that's why I sound so bad, though frankly speaking I don't see what's sexist in the story. She did not care where I came from, I should learn to be sensitive.

I became sensitive, or at least hypocritical. I avoided sexual themes in my stories; in public, I pretended not to notice sexy women, even if they were nearly naked. And I wondered how people would take my next story. I wrote the threesome story, "Under Her Thumb," and mailed it to male editors. Right away David Bradley accepted the story for *New Virginia Review*. At the time, he gave public readings from one of his novels, mostly the chapters about visiting whorehouses. There was a sympathetic ear. He wanted me to make some minor revisions. Together with the revisions, I sent him another story, which I thought was not as good as "Thumb." Bradley wrote to me: You've spoiled everything. We put so much work into your first story, and now you send us a better one. We'll take the better one.

After that, "Under Her Thumb" got rejected at thirty places, by male and female editors alike, by literary and pornographic magazines.

The story even occasioned some trouble for me in my marriage. When my wife found it among my papers at the Fine Arts Work Center in Provincetown, she said, Did you do that?

Yes, I wrote the story.

I mean that filthy sex, did you do it?

No of course not, it's fiction. Otherwise, I'd call it a memoir.

But she was upset, and didn't believe me. She said, Look, many of your stories are autobiographical, you told me.

Well, this one isn't.

On the sly, I mailed the story to several more editors, and showed it to several women writers, who found it a fertile ground for applying Marxist and feminist theories. The story had sexploitative elements. The woman is treated in parts, as an object of desire. She's described way too much compared with the men, she's reified.

Now the application of Marxist terminology to feminist criticism did not sound particularly fresh to me. I was desensitized to Marxist terms—they had, through overuse in Yugoslav socialist totalitarianism, grown to be a bunch of clichés.

But despite my dismissing the criticism, it took hold, and while I was rewriting my story (now renamed "Arrival," since I thought the French say, *J'arrive!*) I was self-conscious. How to describe the woman? Silky hair, velvety lips. No, it won't do, I'm using fabrics, constructing a doll.

How about coppery hair, or golden locks of hair, or platinum blonde? No, now I'm doing some kind of industrial metallurgy with precious metals; in addition to everything else, the woman sounds like a commodity. And what's "locks of hair" supposed to mean? Lock, some kind of bondage? No, strike it out.

Ruby lips, pearly white teeth, brilliant smile. No, now I'm making the woman out of precious stones, and out of clichés.

Almond-shaped eyes, hazel-colored eyes, pear-shaped waist, apple-red cheeks, lips like the bud of a moist flower, peachy fuzz on her upper lip. Now I'm making up a woman out of fruits, plants.

She strode like a gazelle. Her snaky waist coiled and uncoiled. Now I'm demeaning the woman, making her into an animal.

On the other hand, you can call a woman a goddess. Aphrodite, Venus, or at least a demi-god, angelic beauty. But these terms were all invariably overused, clichés. In addition, if you call a woman Aphrodite, it might seem like an oblique way of saying that the woman is overweight. I like plump women, although I must admit that my tastes have been thinned down. As a kid, during the mini-skirt era, I admired women's thighs: the bigger the thighs, the more beautiful and exciting to behold. Gradually, I got trained, I guess, through ads, to appreciate thin women too. I agree with feminists in criticizing the thinning down of the ideal women's look as a form of hatred of the female flesh.

Actually, it might be fine to use the Aphrodite image, or a Venus image, if these hadn't been overdone. Moreover, most Venuses in museums are armless and decapitated, for one reason or another—this association could be seen as inimical to women.

What if I simply write, a beautiful woman? No, too general—does not evoke an image. I believe that my writing should be concrete, imagistic, vivid—that's my ideology, or anti-ideology. How can I evoke images without metaphors? Fuzzy thighs, soft lips, shining eyes, sharp eyebrows, graceful clavicles, shimmering black hair. . . curvaceous earlobes. Pretty soon, I get tired; many of these words put together strike me as clichéd, and even if some of them aren't, by now I've slowed down, run out of energy, become so cautious that just introducing a character in an erotic story appears to be an overwhelming task.

Describing men, of course, I run into the same problems—aquiline nose, chiseled features, bullish neck, leonine hair, steely gaze, bronze tan—but somehow the arsenal of clichés and materials for describing men seems smaller. Many feminists are right to claim that the male is on the whole less objectified than the female; the male is treated more frequently as the subject rather than the object. There are far fewer male nude paintings than female, and I seem to have much less interest in describing a male appearance than a female, though I do a poor job at both. In my fiction, I describe people's looks little, for fear of clichés. I describe everything else, but there, it somehow does not seem to matter.

When I move on to sex, the verbs are no less problematic than the nouns and adjectives. Caressed, sighed, sucked, licked, shoved, slid, poked, kissed, fucked, squeezed, groaned, and so on—in fact, there aren't that many verbs to describe sex. And most of these verbs, under my fingers, sound pale and tired. To sound fresher, I might resort to a metaphor. "She rode him, and his abdomen twitched like a whipped horse's flank." Now the man is an animal, the woman is a human person, so that should be fine—women won't jump on me for this, and men don't care, not yet—but the horse image is old, overused.

Maybe this is not altogether bad. Maybe I do have to resort to metaphors and likenesses: no matter what I describe, I usually do resort to likeness, but my doubts creep in, they gallop in—and the doubts certainly don't arouse me, but slow me down, I lose my pace or I never develop it, and my writing remains cramped, not spontaneous.

My writing is neither excited nor exciting, although after dozens of anthologies of feminist erotica (much of it quite graphic) and general anthologies of erotica, I should not feel constrained.

I think that women have cleared the field of erotic writing so that once again men can comfortably write erotica. Men should thank women for liberating us. The basis for the feminist movement was a striving for equality between the sexes. Women can write erotica; therefore, men can write erotica. Or rather, we are allowed to; whether we can is a different issue.

LITERARY TOMBS

ONE DAWN IN 1983, outside of the Prague train station, I stood off-balance on the descending conveyor belt that slid me into the subways with their ceramically ornamented walls. A man in a beret told me that because the subway was built by the Soviets, its cars were so massive that the paintings in the art museum used to fall off the walls whenever a subway train passed beneath it. If I missed the bus, he told me, I could kill time by visiting the large Jewish cemetery, with Kafka's tomb, right opposite my subway exit. When I emerged from the underground—where the dead rather than the living could be commuting—I did miss the bus.

I rubbed my eyelids and tried to look to the cemetery through the pain with which the brilliant sun afflicted my eyes. When I walked through the gate, cool shade soothed my eyes. Large black marble tombstones, untailored evergreen trees, shocks of grass, dank soil. In many places the branches hung low, touching the tombs marked with Hebrew and German inscriptions. I walked through the shaggy graveyard alleys, back and forth, one by one, and then along a wall, more aware of the stickiness of my socks than of the wall that shielded the cemetery from the street and the street from the cemetery— the passersby from the dead and the dead from the passersby.

The light brown-gray stones of the wall were dark in places, probably from coal smoke.

On my left remained the darkness of trees and tombs. Suddenly whiteness burst at me. I narrowed my eyes to be able to look at it. My eyelids refracted the light, which tremblingly showed me the letters from the stone, FRANZ KAFKA. The blackness of the trees and nearby stones grew green, the white tombstone pulsated with the blood of my eyes. The warmth of the sun and the light dizzied me and lightened me, but one thing was still needed to perfect the experience: I took off my shoes and my socks so nothing would separate my soles from the soil, and rubbed my bare toes against each other over dust and gravel; my skin rejoiced in the coldness of the ground, and I relished my dizziness as if it were a communication from the dead beneath the stone. Behind me, when I turned around, was the plaque of Max Brod, without whom Kafka would have remained unknown and free from the visits of the likes of me. And though I disliked any presence behind me, I felt as though a conspirator was there with me—a memory hunter.

Soon, with my socks and shoes back on, I walked to my bus stop, happy that I had been stunned by the tombstone, aware that the experience offered itself to easy embellishment and fabrication. I wished to have more experiences like that one.

And so, as some letter writers begin to collect stamps, I began to collect memories of graveyard visits; and as many philatelists specialize in stamps of certain regions and themes, I began to specialize in visits to the graves of the famous Continental writers, not heeding Bulatovich's epigram— "There were many people at the cemetery, mostly grieving relatives and bad poets."

In Leningrad, nevertheless, I wanted to visit the tomb of Dostoyevski, but my tour guide did not know where it was, and though I walked up and down Nevsky Prospect many times, I was not aware that at the end of the street reposed the writer in Tikhni Cemetery.

In 1988, in Weimar with a friend of mine, a mathematician awaiting his East German exit visa, I was determined to visit the Goethe mausoleum. On the way to the Stadtpark with the mausoleum, I hesitated, facing three men who humbly waited for me to step off the bus first. They wore blue worker's suits. Their deeply creased skin was pale and transparently red, their eyes livid blue, pained and unmoved; they looked like a Dürer drawing, like engraved seals of an old nation, which, when you face them, imprint themselves on you, sealing a document of some sort through the used yellowness of your retina. I could hear the stamping of iron facing them.

Wow! I said to my friend Detlev, who replied, *Berger*. How do you say it in English?

Miners.

On the way, we had a sip of bitter coffee in Goethe Cafe, passed by a yellow Goethe museum and by an orange Goethe gymnasium. As we entered the Stadtpark with the Goethe mausoleum, I asked: How come this park is not called Goethe Park?

Because there is a bigger park, which is!

The ground was covered by green and red crumpled leaves, writhing and rustling in the wind.

The ceiling of the mausoleum dome was blue with a few gilded stars and long rays. In the middle of the gray marble stone a fence surrounded an opening; through a grating I saw two rectangular varnished wooden boxes. *Faust's Night* lines, the only ones I could remember from the book, occurred to me. "I have studied philosophy, jurisprudence, and medicine, and alas, theology, with great zeal, and here, I stand once more, no wiser than before."

And I stood, as bored as before: nothing special. But wait, I thought, it might come yet. We walked down the stairs.

How do you say, *Gruft*? asked Detlev.

Mausoleum, I told you!

No, Mao is in a mausoleum, Lenin too, there you can see the body.

Here we can see the coffin.

No, it cannot be a mausoleum!

I felt like telling him, Shut up, I want to have a concentrated experience of visiting a famous ghost, not quarrel over words.

The coffins were not much to look at, so I began to look around into the darkness. All along the walls were black dusty boxes, crowded together like worthless materials in a factory outlet, and above them a tarnished plaque hung with the names of dukes of Weimar, duchesses, counts and countesses. It was the mausoleum of the dukes of Weimar, one of whom had invited Goethe to be buried alongside him if he so wished. Probably he hadn't planned it the way it turned out: he, pushed against the wall in a dusty coffin, Goethe, elevated in the center in a polished one—a rude guest even in death! In life, Goethe probably wasn't rude, but imposing; and that his name covered so many places in Germany is doubtless to be attributed to his political genius at least as much as to his literary genius. As a vice-councillor and a friend of many influential people, he had his fingers in all sorts of projects; for example, he supervised the rebuilding of the Weimar Palace though he was not an architect, and he designed the Weimar Park (now Goethe Park) though he was not an urban designer or landscaper, and though many who were competed for the projects. Goethe was rich. On the other hand, Schiller (I notice I have made the mistake I'm criticizing—of allotting all the space to Goethe, the attention magnet) died a pauper and was buried in a communal grave, so that it is not certain that the bones in the coffin with Schiller's name are indeed Schiller's.

Goethe willed that Schiller be buried with him, so some pauper's bones, perhaps Schiller's, were undug, cleaned, and placed into a coffin next to Goethe's. And here they were, one soul in two bodies—that's how Goethe had defined friendship, after some Ancient. Actually, one soil in two coffins, and two coffins in one grave, is what the friendship now amounted to. Fresh carnations, red and white, were in front of the coffins, as though the men had just been buried, although they had not been buried. It struck me as strange—somehow naked, mutilated—that the bones of the two men, elevated in coffins above the stone floor, were isolated from the soil below. Shouldn't your bones be in the earth rather than above it once you died? Shouldn't your stuff go back into the mother earth, rather than be cut away in a monstrous stone imitation of a womb?

On the way back, at the edge of Goethe Park, we visited airy Liszt's house with creaking floors, examined the scratchy handwritings of Schumann and Brahms, gazed at the tranquility and dignity of Liszt's *Totenmask* raised next to a sunny window, and shuddered at the sight of Beethoven's *Totenmask*—the head shrunken, cheeks sunk, small upper teeth protruding from his thinned lips; terror, rage, disease. I wondered, What is Beethoven's mask doing in Liszt's house, on a lower shelf in a corner?

In a walk alongside a pine forest on our left, my brother and I admired the greenery of the descending slope on our right, the hazy dark gray-blue of the Zurich lake, and the hill beyond the lake that echoed the shape and size of the hill we stood on. To the tolling of distant sheep, he told me that in addition to the beauty of nature and culture, the area boasted Thomas Mann's grave, whereupon I livened up from my dusky slumber and insisted that we see the grave without delay.

Since my brother didn't know where exactly the grave was, we wandered and read the names in the cemetery. There were many Schweitzers, and no doubt many talented corpses, but I wanted only Mann's. We couldn't find the tomb, and, jumping over the cemetery fence to cut the distance, my brother promised when I visited again, he would have the grave ready for me. But he didn't. Next month we went into the cemetery, and the search resumed. Ivan led me to the central plateau of the yard, with many flowers and white gravel. The first tombstone I laid my eyes upon read THOMAS MANN. We rushed to the stone as if there was danger of it vanishing. There were fresh flowers in two pots on the sides of the precisely yet roughly hewn large cubic stone. The name of Mann's wife was beneath his. In front of the block of stone were smaller stones, laid down in the grass, with the names of their children. There was no cross, no symbol engraved on the stones.

On our way back, staring at a huge black clock with gilded Roman numbers and gilded limbs on the small cemetery chapel, I weighed the last experience, comparing it with the visit to Kafka's grave, which was wonderful, and to Goethe's and Schiller's, which was not much during my visit, but which had grown in the meantime to the status of a striking experience; and I wondered whether the quiet impression of the cubic stone would grow in my memory. Had I become too promiscuous, each visit to the dead meaning less and less? As we climbed away from the cemetery through cow dung and grass, the clock beat time with rich brass echoes, and I feared I would remember the sound more than the sight of Mann's grave.

But it was because of this fear that nothing remarkable would remain after seeing the graves of famous writers—and that I could not trust my memory to last—that I decided to write about visiting the graves.

In Hollywood, people drive around to stare at the villas of living movie stars, but in Paris, the dead make for the best stargazing scene. At the entrance to the Père Lachaise Cimetière, people stood in line to buy stargazing maps. At Balzac's grave there were fresh yellow carnations, and above the stone, there was no cross, but Balzac's head. So, here he is, dead at fifty, after more than fifty novels, fifteen cups of coffee a day, perpetual schemes to run away from creditors, with no reliable address. Now, a hundred years later, the address could not be more reliable. On the side of the grave were the letters of Comtesse Rzewuska, his Polish mistress/wife. Nobody was visiting the grave during my five-minute stay. Next to his grave was a tomb with a little chapel, grave of a painter who died at twenty-five. Through the blue-stained glass, sunshine streaked and hit red and brown leaves, which floated by in a hush.

On the way to Chopin's grave, I passed by the central chapel, where a service was taking place, with a dirge played out slowly. Black cabs stood parked outside, and the drivers smoked cigarettes impatiently. Wreaths of flowers with purple ribbons covered the steps, and inside, people walked around the coffin. A woman walked out and wept, and leaned against the chapel walls.

From the chapel I walked down, and in a narrow alley found Chopin's grave, with many wreaths, flowers, and ribbons. The largest ribbon bore the inscription, Polish Embassy. There was a Polish flag here. A couple in black came by and whispered and crossed themselves and laid down white roses.

Not far from this one, I saw a crowd. I guessed it must be Jim Morrison's grave, and when I came close enough, I could read James. . . Morrison. (There was a middle name too, but James already sounded odd.) The grave was in a back row, several yards away from the alleys. A front row grave plot costs about eight thousand dollars, a back row plot around four thousand. It's always possible to buy a slot here because the cemeteries destroy the graves that are no longer visited. Supposedly, if a grave has not had flowers on it for more than a year, and nobody calls to claim it, the management removes the stone and sells the plot to a new customer. So, although the cemetery bore the names of close to a hundred thousand people, more than a million lay here underfoot. The Morrison estate certainly could have afforded the front row, but perhaps the French government did not want him to have it because even in the back rows, his presence was rowdy enough. About two dozen youngsters smoked pot, wept, shouted, and attempted to write graffiti on adjacent stones, but a guard who stood nearby warned them not to do it. The comparison between the number of visits to Morrison's grave and Balzac's could sufficiently attest that the serious novel may be dead or in a critical condition, but rock is alive. And Balzac's grave was no anomaly. Nobody was at Proust's grave. I stood at his black marble stone, two graves removed from an alley; the stone was smooth, shiny, low to the ground, looking as new as if it had been planted the day before.

At the avenue walked a young sorrowful woman with a bodice lower than her skirt. She exchanged glances with me and walked on to the crematorium, slowly, with a sensuous amble, appropriate near Proust's grave. A thought crossed my mind that the cemetery could be a meat market of Paris, although I was sure that the thought was unfair to the young woman. Still, I recalled a story by Maupassant, "Graveyard Sisterhood," in which a prostitute picks up customers at Montmartre cemetery. "Was it a profession—a graveyard sisterhood who walked the cemeteries . . .? Or had she alone hit upon that admirable idea, that profoundly philosophical notion, of exploiting the amorous regrets awakened in those mournful places?"

And it was Maupassant's grave I wanted to see next, but for this I had to visit the Montparnasse cemetery. For my essay it would have been better if he had been buried at the Montmartre cemetery, which he had described at length in "Graveyard Sisterhood," lyrically and thoughtfully, yet he ended up in the flat-walled cemetery of Montparnasse, far from the cemetery avenues. It took me a while to locate his grave, close to a cedar and next to a Legion of Honor soldier. It was a high stone, resembling the frame of a gate. On the soil there were flowers, I did not pay attention to their kind. After two years of syphilitic dementia, he ended up here. His grave was visited. A large family, seeing me there, rushed to the grave—it insulted me that they took me for a tourist rather than for a mourner, although I was not in the least in a mournful mood—and they spoke in excited Polish. Did Maupassant's influence spread eastward better than westward? Isaac Babel wrote a great story, "My Maupassant," and Russians used to hold Maupassant, as the short story master, in higher regard than Chekhov.

From here I walked on to the other section of the graveyard, over Rue Emile Richard. Workers were smashing a gravestone and throwing the stones into a dump truck. Clearly, nobody had mourned on that grave in a while, and the space was precious. I found Beckett's grave, and wondered what would be the appropriate cynical response, in the spirit of his work, whether to take a leak or sit bored, but when I noticed that his wife too lay buried there, out of respect for her I did not opt for the former. She died soon after him, perhaps of grief. Could it be that the cynic had a happy marriage? Somebody had glued several yellow willow leaves on the stone. I walked over to another happy couple, Sartre and S. de Beauvoir. They too had plenty of flowers, yellow for some reason, and no cross, of course, unlike Baudelaire, around the corner and alone. There was a sea of flowers here. Were they a pun of sorts, les fleurs du mal? The cold rain and a whipping wind forced me to reconsider the worth of my visit—wouldn't it be morbid to become gravely ill at a cemetery? I was contributing nothing to the guys in the ground, and to be with them, I decided I should better leave the dank winds and stay home and read—have the thoughts of the dead relived in me. No, this was not a conversion—I hoped to visit more continental, transcontinental, as well as incontinent corpses of writers, but for now, the cumulative effect of my spending two half-days among the graves was a malaise and a sense of alienation, a feeling—nothing literary—that comes upon me after being in any cemetery for too long.

A couple of weeks later, Ivo and I went to Fluntern Cemetery in Zurich, near the zoo, to see Joyce's grave. It was a rainy Sunday, and the blue tram #5 took us to the cemetery at its last stop. It was a relatively new cemetery, from the end of the last century, a bay of grass cutting into an evergreen hill. The intense rain created a haze and a low pressure, so that in tranquility we yawned. If there had been a dry piece of ground with pine needles I could have sprawled over it and fallen asleep right there. The graves in the center section were spacious, with single files of large cobbles making paths aside from the main path. Most graves had candle flames in red glass containers with a hole on the side for oxygen, so that the rain could not extinguish the fire. Now we took a look at the cemetery map. There were less than a dozen entries here—for the mass grave, the chapel, and James Joyce. Joyce was the only individual named. No need for a map here. Arrows pointed the way to him. He had become a tourist trap. Up at the highest point of the cemetery, behind hedges, stood his grave, or rather, sat Joyce, that is, his sculpture. I had seen the sculpture in many textbooks, and I had not known that that was the gravestone. There was no cross here, Joyce's God must be Joyce, or one of our gods was Joyce. He sat in bronze, his legs crossed, left ankle over the right knee, and at his right side leaned a walking stick. (My brother commented that I should take a photo of the grave, so I could describe it accurately. That's true, I said, the descriptions would be better, but I'd

probably carry on too long, and anyway, the photo arts are
the enemy of the literary arts. One picture equals a thousand
words, so why bother with words?) Joyce's feet were amazingly
narrow—either Giacometti's influence, or, if this was a realistic
presentation of Joyce's feet, it probably had to do with Italian
shoes. He lived in Italy long enough to have his feet squeezed
by the Italian shoe industry. Mine, from living in a neighboring
country, certainly were—even now my left foot hurt because
I'd walked most of my adolescence in narrow Italian shoes. On
James's head (it feels odd to call him by his first name, and
would be odder to say Jim Joyce, but why not?) was some white
stuff, at first I thought a present from the pigeons, but it turned
out to be cold candle wax, in a circle. Somebody must have
burned a candle atop his head. Water drops burst on his skull,
and water dripped down his glasses, and his lips, onto his lap.
The plaque on his grave was covered by yellow cedar needles,
and to read it, I removed them with my fingertips. *Gebornen in
Dublin. . . Gestorben in Zurich*. Why was he buried in German?
Next to his grave was a small willow, perhaps a bonsai, but a
little too large for a bonsai, and a little too small for a real
willow. The bumpy tree squatted and bent its branches. Joyce
looked thoughtful, and his gaze fell—and stayed fallen—upon
a fresh grave, with orange flowers, not cut, but growing from
the ground in a multitude. The grave bore a thin varnished
orange cross. Elias Canetti. He had died in August 1994, and
this was November, no time for a stone yet. Canetti liked to
write about death and cemeteries, as did Joyce.

At any rate, in the haze of rain and mist I had no epiphany,
although I remembered the last snowy lines of *The Dead*: "It
was falling, too, upon every part of the lonely churchyard on
the hill where Michael Furey lay buried. It lay thickly drifted
on the crooked crosses and headstones, on the spears of the
little gate, on the barren thorns. His soul swooned slowly as he
heard the snow falling faintly through the universe and faintly

falling, like the descent of their last end, upon all the living and the dead." Could you substitute rain for snow, and have the same effect? Why does snow seem to be so much more expressive than rain? Maybe I should visit here when it snows, although there could be no crooked cross in this tidy Swiss cemetery, unless Joyce's body could be taken for one. At any rate, to form my impression, I would have to make do with the cold hushing rain, and that did not cheer me, as my shoes soaked up the cold. My eyeballs grew cold in the vapors. The vapors drifted upon the softened face of the earth, collected the last breaths left in the soil, lifted them, and took them into the pine woods, sifting them through the needles.

On the way home, Ivo and I visited the Zurich Public Library and its reading room. The walls were lined with journal shelves. I found several dozen literary journals from the States, including the *Joyce Quarterly* and other Joyce journals, as well as several magazines with my stories in them. It was clear that people were not rushing to the shelves. In fact, I'd never seen anybody in a library pick up a small literary journal. The journals stood here, like thin urns, ashes of reticence. And if I wrote about the grave visits, the scriptoral aftermath of the visits would—at best—end up along the walls, unread, unmoved, silent, buried at a few libraries. That would be fine and appropriate.

BALKAN EXPRESS

MAY 25, 2010, IN ZAGREB, I walked up to the ticket hall at Glavni Kolodvor, dreading long lines in front of the international counter. Here I had bought my ticket to Paris when I left Yugoslavia for good; and at the same counter I had bought my first ticket abroad when I was seventeen, to London (which almost explains why this essay is in English). Twenty, thirty, and more years ago, at the same station, there were long angry lines in front of three international counters. Now there was only one counter and no line. I asked the relaxed, wide-eyed saleswoman for the schedule and pricing to Sofia.

You are curious or you want to buy? she asked.

Of course I want to buy. How much is it?

Most people only ask and then go away. It's 328 *kunas*.

Not much at all! To fly would be 328 dollars, six times more. Should I get a sleeping car?

I wouldn't. You can probably have a whole row of seats to yourself—most likely a whole compartment.

And how much would a first class ticket be?

Twice as much, but there's no difference between second and first class. The first class cars are so old they are sometimes worse than the second class, and anyway you can always buy a first class ticket on the train if you feel like impressing yourself.

OK, I'll get a one-way fare. Why does it say *brzi* and not express?

It's too slow to be called express any more.

I hopped on the train at half past midnight. The train was an hour late because it was held up at the Slovenian-Croatian border, and it took nearly seven hours to get to Belgrade. This trip used to take only four hours on the express. I wondered why no trains could be express any more, and strangely enough the man who sat with me in the compartment turned out to be a train engine man going home to Novska, and he explained that the tracks needed maintenance, that some were uneven, and at higher speeds they could cause oscillation, which would threaten derailment. So from Zagreb to Banova, we could go at 80km max, 100 from Banova to Novska, then 120 till Slavonski Brod, 160 until Vinkovci, and then the speed in Serbia would gradually go back down to 80 km, and between Sid and Belgrade, 50 km.

By the way, the engine man said, as he stood up to leave the train in Novska. Close the window or you will get a nasty cold.

Oh really? I said. *Propuh*?

Jeste, he said.

But it was a warm day.

It's chilly now.

I had some trepidation during the blue dawn before the border. For years I had imagined this moment, especially during the war. Would they have me in the books because I had written critically against the Serbian regimes? Why would they?

I have two passports but I prefer to travel on the American one, for some reason. Considering the NATO bombing of Belgrade, a Croatian passport might look better at the Serbian border, but nevertheless, I pulled out the US passport. The police on the Croato-Serbian border were polite, both Serbian and Croatian, giving me no trouble whatsoever.

In Sid, a lean and dignified man in a suit came in, and talked incredibly dirty, *Jebem ti!* My dear Sir, just look out the window, it's all fucked up, all this fucking garbage.

I haven't noticed.

What pigs we are, fucked up the whole damned country and we keep throwing garbage all over this shithole.

Oh, it's not all that bad, I said.

Yes, it is. You know, just a few days ago I visited this lovely town in Croatia, Daruvar, you probably never heard of it: clean streets, flowers, polite people, some speaking Czech.

I didn't tell him that used to be my hometown. I wished him good luck.

I changed trains in Belgrade. The train station used to be so crowded that you couldn't walk out from the platform without jostling. I went to a kiosk and bought a bottle of water and then walked to a little grocery shop, where I bought two cold beers, Niksicko pivo. The clerk wanted to bill me for the water too and didn't believe that I had already bought it at another store. Wonderful, she is accusing me of shoplifting water. I told her it was absurd, and she said, Sorry, you never know. People will steal anything.

I bought a *burek,* an old taste of Yugoslavia—sourdough in oil and cheese. And I drank a cold beer even though it was eight in the morning. My throat was dry because of not sleeping the previous night. The beer didn't taste great, and I washed away the taste of the first with the second bottle. We started with only a twenty-minute delay, through Belgrade and south. I wished I had enough time to visit some old friends of mine and to take a walk, to remember the old days when I used to visit as a medical student from Novi Sad, 80 km north of the city.

The scenery outside of the train was, of course, scenic, along the Morava River—red poppy fields, peasants tilling the soil, snow in the distance in the mountains, and along the tracks there were abandoned cargo coaches with hay and weeds in them; some weeds grew through the floorboards.

I had hoped to get a story out of the trip, and I was not getting it. There were no strange encounters on the train. I had written several stories with strange encounters on trains. I had never visited Serbia before without having some strange experience, and the only strange experience I had now was that I was not having any. The train was extremely slow as it ascended into the mountains toward Bulgaria. The Serbian border patrol at Dimitrovgrad was far from the image of a militaristic state. A fashionably dressed policewoman in a blue miniskirt, black stockings, and high heels asked for our passports. She was more interested in her make-up, which she checked in the mirror above me, than in my passport. Later she sat with the train signal-man on a bench, crossing her legs becomingly, like a TV hostess, and the signal-man, talking vivaciously, forgot to wave the train away for a few minutes: there is no other explanation why we were at a standstill.

We moved slowly, a kilometer or so. The Bulgarian police came. Bulgarians, from my experience, seem to be the friendliest people in the Balkans, idiotic as it is to generalize, so I was happy to see them after the Serbian police. One policeman stamped the passport slowly and gently, as though afraid to hurt the paper.

He left, and I thought how decent the police in Europe were about border crossing. In Canada and the States, when you cross, they tend to ask you how long you are going to stay, why, where, how, how much money you carry, and so on. Even personal questions, like Who are your friends? What do they do? Why are they your friends? What do you do with them?

Just as I marveled at how decent the Bulgars were, asking no intrusive questions, the policeman came back and asked, Why are you going to Bulgaria?

I am going to promote a book of mine which came out in translation.

You have a book? he said, and grinned. His teeth were white and good, other than one apparently dead tooth, which was blue.

Have a nice stay in Bulgaria!

No story. That's good. I don't want border crossing stories. I have written too many and they blend together now as a boring genre.

Meanwhile, a man with several different pairs of pliers, a hammer, and a wedge was checking the roof in the corridor. He took out one board. A policeman with a camera took pictures of the space between the roof and the boards. One policeman carried a submachine gun. They went down the length of the car in both directions, taking plastic boards off the roof, fumbling in search of something, perhaps not people. . . maybe they were looking for drugs. Now and then they passed by my compartment, asked nothing, looked in briefly above me and below me.

Another policeman showed up and walked into my compartment and asked, You also have a Serbian passport, don't you?

Why? I don't look American to you?

You have a Serbian passport.

No, Croatian. Nobody asked me about multiple passports before.

How long will you stay in Bulgaria?

For a week.

Why Bulgaria? There are many more interesting countries, Greece, Croatia.

Just imagine if they found drugs. Who would they blame? The British kids in the first two compartments, who walked around barefoot? The handful of people who had just come on board? Or me, on the train since Zagreb? Some drugs arrive at Croatian ports and travel north through Hungary or Austria into Germany for large-scale consumption. Of course it would make sense to beat the expected route and to go south, enter the EU zone at the least expected spot. Once in Bulgaria, the drugs could travel north. With the ensuing interrogation and beatings and a few other adventures, I could get a whole book out of the experience; should I hope that they find drugs and drag me out and give me some valuable experience, such as an MFA cannot buy but a bit of heroin can? Well, maybe it would be painful, but still not a book's worth of self-pity. There are poppies in the fields, a stork on an electrical relay station, wonderfully red poppy fields—why so many? I love poppy seed pies and poppy seed bagels. . . does any of it end up as heroin? Opium?

What will I do if they blame me? Will they arrest me? Who would I call? How would I prove I was innocent? Could it be like Mexico where. . . I kept imagining the story, and it was getting larger and more threatening. Now the train was two hours late. The trip—or journey at this point?—would be nineteen hours long, at best. I would not make it to the reception in Sofia on time. But that did not worry me.

No, this is not the story I wanted to write, and actually, luckily, it is a story I don't have to write. The cops put the roof back together, walked out of the train, hopped into a jeep, and were gone. The station master came out and waved his little round sign loosely. Did he raise it enough to count as a go-ahead? Yes, the train moved and I felt relieved that I was not going to be arrested as a drug trafficker. Maybe they could arrest me as a trafficker in stories?

The train was passing by shepherds herding goats, goatherds. . . What's the point of herding goats? To protect them from others, or to protect vegetables from the goats? To whip them if they stray toward the grapes? Looking through the window, I began to cough. What the hell? Did sleeplessness and beer get me? Or am I allergic to heroin dust or something floating through the train? Or did that famous Balkan *promaja*, or *propuh*, get me in Croatia and then in Nis? The engine man warned me well. My bronchi felt congested, wheezy. I coughed and thought, Shit, this will ruin my swimming.

At the next station, very few people boarded the train. The train seemed almost dead, running at a loss to all the governments involved, a relic. I am not usually sentimental about things, but this train filled me with nostalgia; its emptiness filled me with malaise. I missed the old Balkan express (and Orient Express, Simplon Express, and other express trains on the same route), with its pickpockets, live chickens, soldiers, Inter-Rail hordes of northern European children, women sitting on their large disks of cheese on the way to Nis farmer's market. . . it used to be a world, a bustling street stretching from Munich to Istanbul, full of alleyways, private spaces, flirtation, threats, envy, classes, . . . a multinational train, but all that multinationality didn't save the multinational country, Yugoslavia, and the death of Yugoslavia was partly responsible for the death of this train. For nearly ten years there was no continuous traffic between Croatia and Serbia; the tracks aged, the coaches deteriorated. I remember visiting some coaches that had been sidelined as a refugee camp near Vinkovci, Vagonsko naselje, after the siege of Vukovar, but now many of those coaches were rusted on overgrown tracks, completely useless back in Croatia, just as the coaches were useless in Serbia. The war not only destroyed the walking culture—as people stayed indoors for a couple of years, afraid of shelling, and so lost the habit—it also destroyed the trains.

Oh, it cannot be all that bad, I thought. It could be worse. The train is still here and maybe it will come back to life and people will have fantastic experiences.

At one point, just a week before this trip, I wanted to go from Zagreb to my hometown, Daruvar, by train, and not just for sentimental reasons. The train had been cheaper than the bus when I had visited the year before. And for me, the train was an image of freedom: freedom to leave and freedom to come back. I had left my home valley for the first time on a steam-engine train, and for years I kept traveling back and forth between Daruvar and Zagreb and Vinkovci and Virovitica smelling coal and steam. I loved to lean out of the window in the smoke and steam of the engine train, and even the little particles of coal that smarted my face gave me a sensation of adventure and freedom. The first sustained conversation I had in English took place on a train, from Rome to Vienna, almost the entire trip.

I talked to my brother on the phone, telling him I was going to find an evening train to get to Daruvar.

He laughed. There's no evening train.

Fine, I'll come tomorrow morning. Don't they have a ridiculously early train, at 5:55?

You remember well. No, there is no morning train either. There is no train to Daruvar at all. The line is abolished.

Why? They are fixing the tracks or something?

No, they had the funeral for the last train just last month.

What do you mean, funeral?

I mean funeral. They retired the last train. People marched behind it, and the brass band played the funeral march. People put wreaths of flowers on it, some wept, and then we all went home. It was like burying your grandfather. It was a rainy day, too.

But that's absurd. Why didn't they save the train? (Here, I coughed. Or maybe I didn't, how could I remember coughing as punctuation, but I coughed during the conversation in places.)

The train was losing money, Vlado elaborated. It was nearly always empty, and instead of getting faster, it was getting slower because the state didn't want to repair the tracks.

So how do the poor travel?

By bus, and most people have cars anyway. And some just don't travel.

Another question that crossed my mind was how people would commit suicide now. The train used to be the most popular form of suicide. The mother of a friend of mine killed herself when he was twelve by lying on the tracks before the train. Another mother failed and lost her arm under the wheels. I suppose cargo trains could be used, but their schedule is not so regular, and maybe the regularity was comforting—you could choose the time of your death. (Actually, I found out that the rails were completely defunct, and the cargo train traffic had ceased as well. In some sections of abandoned railways, people steal the rails for the steel.) Maybe suicide would be more American now, using guns as the primary means of transportation to the other world. And nearly everybody had guns now, after the wars.

Now, of course, many American towns went through this—the loss of passenger train connections. But in the Balkans? After all, the main feature of Austrian and Hungarian colonization of the Northern Balkans, including Bosnia, was an intricate system of railways. The Austrians were backward in many ways, but they took pride in building train tracks, and while theirs were better they still gave us good trains. The distinction between superb rails and good rails was kind of an indication of where Europe ceased and its subcontinent, the Balkans, began. After crossing into the Balkans, the rails sounded louder, the clanking between the gaps was jolty, but still smoother than what I would later find in the States and Russia. How can you tell now where the subcontinent begins? I took a road trip from Budapest to Zagreb, and the only thing that changed at the border into Croatia was that the roads became better, smoother. The borders are lost.

God, a whole era has passed. And not only the war is to

blame. Still, one of the most vivid images I have with me of this retired train is one from 1992. Late at night, my friend Boris and I stood by the tracks and the train passed with orange lights in all its windows but not a single passenger head to be seen. Where are the passengers? I asked. The train is empty?

Oh, they are there, you just don't see them. They're on the floor. There used to be snipers all along the tracks and so there are stretches of the rails where people all lie down on the floor so they won't be shot.

Well, now in peace the train is dead, and the Balkan Express is gravely ill. The Orient Express no longer runs. I recommend prayers. Dear Reader, hop onto the train for the last ride if you can, and the last ride might thus be delayed.

ACKNOWLEDGMENTS

These essays stem from many places and encounters with friends, family, and strangers. I would like to thank them all, and especially my friends Jeff Parker, Dan Wickett, Steve Gillis, Richard Burgin, Resa Alboher, Sasa Drach, Hilda Raz, Melvin Bukiet, Larry Wright, Francine Prose, Phil Lopate, Terrence Malick, Mikhail Iossel, David Stromberg, Johnik Goldbach, two Steven Dunns, one and only Boris Beric, and others whom I have tormented with my manuscripts over the years and who have given me provocative advice.

I am grateful to Yaddo, Civitella Ranieri, Concordia University in Montreal, Fulbright Commission, Guggenheim Foundation, Hermitage Artists Retreat, Vogelstein Fund, Norton Island/ Eastern Frontier, and Blue Mountain Center for giving me time and space for writing and in some cases time and space for running away from writing into international geography.